NAHANNI THEN AND NOW

EARLY PRAISE

Why not head up an abandoned road last maintained when the town of Tungsten was left behind lock, stock, and barrel by all inhabitants, decades before? Why not? Viv Lougheed's rollicking tales of adventure on the Nahanni River are the next best thing to being on the trail with her. (Take it from one who knows, that is a very good thing indeed). It is a treat to settle in with her insouciant descriptions of crossing a stomach-deep, fast-flowing river—the kind of danger to life and limb people like her think of as fun—to eavesdrop on her muttered complaints when her companions decide to pack up, and to take the history of the place in digestible spoonfuls. Despite the lightness of her prose, Lougheed's respect for the wilderness is indicated by the fact she has survived this long.

The history of the Nahanni River and its storied environs—the town of Tungsten, abandoned but pristine ever since the mine closed down, or the Cirque of the Unclimbables, a name guaranteed to goad any mountaineer—is here recounted with verve and panache. But Viv Lougheed's tale is enlivened and emboldened by the author's accounts of her own expeditions in the region. Whether trailed by her long-suffering husband, misled by inadvertently unhelpful park staff, or joined by an intrepid gang of fellow hikers, Lougheed frolics enthusiastically with grizzly bears, scales bulldozer-sized boulders that teeter at a touch, throws muttered tantrums when her companions refuse to stay another rain-soaked minute, and nonchalantly crosses a raging, chest-high river where one slip means you're swept away. You'll marvel at her idea of a good time. Depending on your disposition, you'll either decide with husband John that home is where the dry roof is or hope to be invited to the next wine-soaked planning session. Whether you're an armchair traveller or a heli-hiker like her, Lougheed brings you on her treks to the majestic places few of us will ever see in a lifetime, let alone return to again and again over the course of a 40-year backcountry hiking career.

CARELLIN BROOKS
Award winning author of numerous titles including Wreck Beach.

She had walked the Great Wall of China and the Inca trail in Peru, and had climbed to lofty mountain villages in Tibet. In a column she wrote weekly for the Prince George Citizen, Vivien extolled the virtues of strapping on a pair of boots and taking to the great outdoors.

WAYNE ROSTAD from On the Road Again TV series

The grande dame of English language travel writers heads out of bounds on almost every trip she's ever taken the world over, and in Nahanni Then And Now she takes the reader well past the mechanics of hiking through one of the world's great far-north landscapes.

FRANK PEEBLES
Writer-Performer-Critic

Vivien Lougheed knows the North from first hand experience scrambling over alpine passes, crossing raging mountain streams and venturing far beyond the beaten trail. Her lively descriptions and personal accounts of these incredible adventures brings out the spirit of exploring the unknown. Indeed Viv's personality is a perfect match to her writings, a walk on the wild side of life! Her latest book, Nahanni Then and Now sheds light on the fascinating history of this renowned land of legends. A great insight into Canada's Northwest!

BRENT LIDDLE
Guide & Park Interpreter, Kluane National Park & Reserve, Yukon

NAHANNI
Then & Now

VIVIEN LOUGHEED

ISBN-13: 978-0-88839-697-6 [trade paperback]
ISBN-13: 978-0-88839-698-3 [epub]
Copyright © 2021 Vivien Lougheed

Library and Archives Canada Cataloguing in Publication

Title: Nahanni : Then & Now / Vivien Lougheed.
Names: Lougheed, Vivien, author.
Description: Includes bibliographical references and index.
Identifiers: Canadiana (print) 20210183675 | Canadiana ebook 20210183772 | ISBN 9780888396976 (softcover) | ISBN 9780888396983 (EPUB)
Subjects: LCSH: Lougheed, Vivien—Travel—Northwest Territories—South Nahanni River Watershed. | LCSH: South Nahanni River Watershed (N.W.T.)—Description and travel. | LCSH: South Nahanni River Watershed (N.W.T.)—History.
Classification: LCC FC4195.S6 L68 2021 | DDC 917.19/3—dc23

All rights reserved. No part of this publication may be reproduced, stored in a retrieval system or transmitted, in any form or by any means, electronic, mechanical, audio, photocopying, recording, or otherwise (except for copying permitted by Sections 107 and 108 of the U.S. Copyright Law and except for book reviews for the public press), without the prior written permission of Hancock House Publishers. Permissions and licensing contribute to the book industry by helping to support writers and publishers through the purchase of authorized editions and excerpts. Please visit www.accesscopyright.ca.

Illustrations and photographs are copyrighted by the artist or the Publisher.

Editor: D. Martens
Production, Cover: J. Rade
Front cover- colour photo of Cathedral Mountain by Linda Thompson
Front/back covers black & white insert - photo taken by Norm Thomas and submitted by Howell Martyn.
All photos in the book are by the author unless otherwise stated.

We acknowledge the financial support of the Government of Canada through the Canada Book Fund and the Canada Council for the Arts, and of the Province of British Columbia through the British Columbia Arts Council and the Book Publishing Tax Credit.

Hancock House gratefully acknowledges the Halkomelem Speaking Peoples whose unceded, shared and asserted territories our offices reside upon.

HANCOCK HOUSE PUBLISHERS LTD.
19313 Zero Avenue, Surrey, B.C. Canada V3Z 9R9
#104-4550 Birch Bay-Lynden Rd, Blaine, WA, U.S.A. 98230-9436
Phone (800) 938-1114   Fax (800) 983-2262
www.hancockhouse.com   info@hancockhouse.com

CONTENTS

Chapter 1: *Mothballed Or Landfilled* 5

Chapter 2: *To Fix a Flat.* 9

Chapter 3: *History Of The Flat Lakes* 27

    George Dalziel 28

    George & Bill Cormack 37

    Nazar Zenchuk 42

Chapter 4: *Discrepancies of the Flat Lake Trappers* 51

Chapter 5: *Traces of Trappers* 57

Chapter 6: *History of Howard's Pass* 63

Chapter 7: *Elsebeth at Howard's Pass 1995* 71

Chapter 8: *History of Union Carbide* 83

Chapter 9: *Union Carbide Hike 1996.* 87

    Furs and Models 95

Chapter 10: *History of Glacier Lake* 99
    Colonel Harry Michener Snyder 103
    Lucy and Hugh Miller Raup, 1939 112
Chapter 11: *The Pentagon Expedition* 121
Chapter 12: *Tungsten to Glacier Lake Hike 1999* 133
Chapter 13: *The Yale Team* 151
Chapter 14: *Winter Research* 163
    Snyder Returns with Flook 164
    Modern Scientists: Donalee Deck 168
Chapter 15: *The Climbing Rush* 173
Chapter 16: *A New Park* 179
Chapter 17: *Glacier Lake/Cirque 2015* 185
    Frost Creek Hike 193
    Food for Common Folks 200
Chapter 18: *Into the Cirque* 203
    Pursuit of the Wall 210
    Jason & Christian 2015 216
    The End 217
Index 219

CONTENTS: NAHANNI

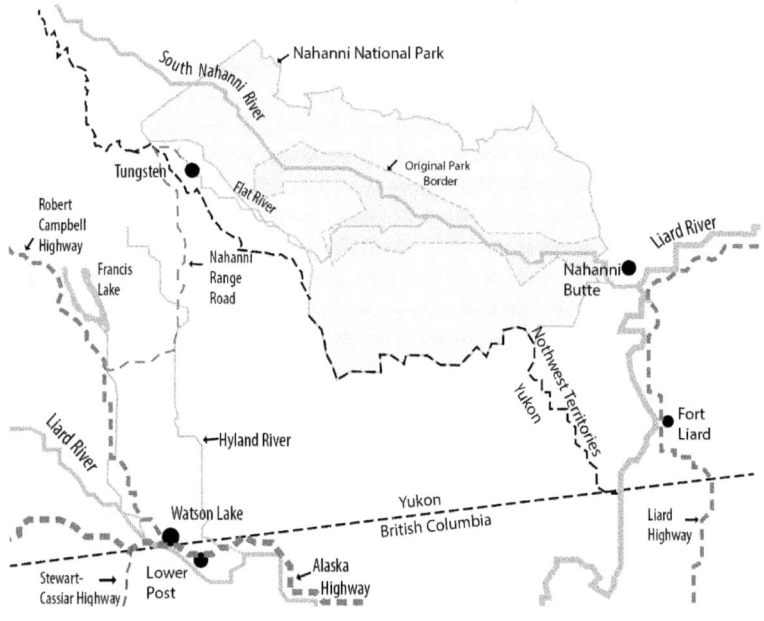

CHAPTER 1

MOTHBALLED OR LANDFILLED

During the cold winter days in early 1993, my husband, John, and I spent hours studying contour maps that indicated possible hiking routes into Nahanni National Park. We'd spent the previous ten years in Kluane National Park, located in the southwest corner of the Yukon, where a half-day's grunt off the Alaska Highway and up a creek got us into the alpine meadows and ice-capped mountains.

Now we wanted something comparable.

I was familiar with the Nahanni River. In the early 1980s, I had talked my friend Joanne Armstrong into paddling the river with me. We'd read R.M. Patterson's book, *Dangerous River*, and Dick Turner's books, *Nahanni* and *Wings of the North*. From there we went to the 1962 National Film Board's presentation about Albert Faille, a legendary hero of the Nahanni. Also, we found a report issued by the Northwest Territories Division of Tourism designed to scare the daylights out of people. It was written by Constable T.E.G. Shaw and it listed all the disappearances investigated by the police in the area since the 1920s.

To add to that, we knew that Pierre Elliot Trudeau, back in power after a short time in the figurative political wilderness, had, in 1972 and during his first term, set out to paddle the river. Even though he canoed only a few miles, the rugged wilderness had inspired him enough to make the area a reserve with park status. During this trip, Trudeau was entertained by Gus and Mary Kraus at the hot springs named after them on the lower South Nahanni River.

Figure Eight Rapids on the Nahanni River. The river's current has changed and the rapids are no longer a danger to paddlers.

Joanne and I had paddled alone, but even with the high standing waves and rushing water that threatened to swamp us, we, too, became enamoured of the rugged wildness and extreme isolation. I wanted to do the river again, but Joanne had retired from adventuring to golf, and John couldn't swim.

Instead, we planned to hike, but we could find just one way of getting close to the park, and that was by accessing the Nahanni Range Road, marked on our contour maps as running from the Robert Campbell highway about a hundred kilometers northwest of Watson Lake. The road crossed the territorial divide into the Northwest Territories and dropped down into a town called Tungsten. The total distance from Watson Lake to the town was less than three hundred kilometers. The map also indicated that there was a hot spring at or near Tungsten.

Dotting off the Nahanni Range Road were lines indicating bulldozed roads; these would keep away the underbrush and make walking possible. We also noticed bridges that would safely allow us to cross what we imagined to be swift, cold and deep streams. And, of interest to John, who liked at least the occasional wall between him and the bears and a roof between him and the rain, were dots representing buildings, with some along the road north of Tungsten, around the Flat Lakes, up the territorial divide and part way to the Canol Road and the headwaters of the South Nahanni river.

John called the RCMP in Watson Lake, who informed him that Tungsten was abandoned, with only a caretaker living there, and that there was a difficult washout to cross part way up the Nahanni Range Road. The rest of the road, he said, had not been maintained since 1986 when the mine had closed. And the town was closed to visitors.

We like to know the histories of places we hike in, how the places came to be, how they survived, why they died. We love poking around abandoned cabins and imagining the lives of those who'd built them and then left.

Our sources of information were mainly mining company reports gleaned from the Vancouver Public Library. As you may recall, 1993 was pre-Internet. The reports told us that, in 1954, a large presence of tungsten had been discovered in Canada's Northwest Territories by Alex Berglund. At the time, he was employed by Northwestern Explorations Ltd. A year later, the company sampled and mapped the find. It turned out to be the second largest deposit in the world, after one in China.

Five years after the discovery, Canada Tungsten Mining Corporation Ltd. (later known as North American Tungsten) was formed. The Nahanni Range Road was built, a mining pit opened and a town was erected for 120 people (27 families). By 1962, the mine, workable only through the summer, was producing 300 tons of ore per day and the ore was milled on site. A year later, the price of tungsten fell and the mine closed. It reopened for a short time and then closed again when the processing mill burned down.

A new mill was completed in 1967, and production resumed. The discovery, in 1971, of a large deposit of tungsten at the north end of town resulted in the digging of an underground mine that could be worked all year. During that period, production rose to 500 tons a day.

By 1979, the population of the town was 506 people. In 1984 a $7 million recreation center was built that contained an Olympic-sized pool, gymnasium, bowling alley, two bars, hair salon, travel agency, dance floor, racquetball court, weight room, shuffleboard tables, tanning salon, hot tub, and library. A medical clinic and curling rink were also added to the town.

Then in the early 1980s, the Chinese, wanting control of the market, sold their tungsten cheaper than Canada could, thus causing financial difficulties for Cantung. To complicate matters, the miners went on strike, demanding more money. Those opposed to the strike claimed that at that time, the miners were among the best paid in North America, each making an average of $100,000 a year, while a junior clerk could count on $60,000. The company subsidized food and housing, so that, as the story goes, it was cheaper to feed dogs T-bone steak than bagged dog food.

After negotiations failed, Cantung shut down the mine and the miners were lucky to have enough time to pack their personal belongings before heading out.

CHAPTER 2

TO FIX A FLAT

As John and I planned our first assault on Nahanni National Park, we realized that any of the likely routes to the famous river would be long and isolated, and we would need help. I conscripted Shea Walsh, an ex-student of mine who was unemployed that summer and eager to get out of the city. He was both smart and strong. We showed him maps and told him only that the trip would include biking to Tungsten and then hiking for three weeks.

After three days of driving from Prince George, we reached Miner's Junction on the Robert Campbell Highway, once a pit stop with a café and gas station and located directly across from the Nahanni Range Road. The bridge north of the junction, crossing the Hyland River, remained useable, but the sign said, "use at your own risk," and the bridge at the Tuchitua River where it crossed the Nahanni Range

Road was washed out, just as the RCMP had told us. The rest of the road had developed sinkholes and would have had to be cleared of boulders if a truck wished to pass.

Miner's Junction on the Robert Campbell Highway at the Nahanni Range Road turnoff.

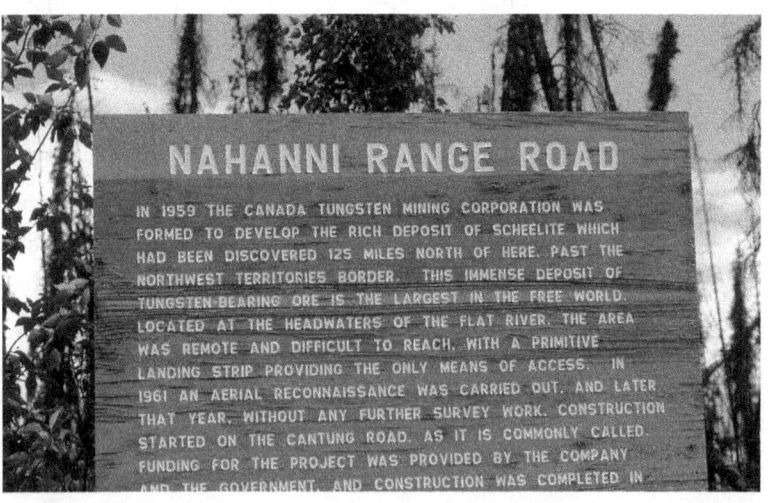

The Nahanni Range Road, commonly called the Cantung Road starts at the Robert Campbell Highway and ends at Tungsten.

At the washout I breathlessly watched John and Shea, bicycles strapped to their backs, struggle against the waist-deep, swift-flowing, glacial water. I held a rope attached to a harness on John's upper body in case he was swept off his feet by the current. Shea was behind him, partly shielded from the water's force by John's wake.

John and Shea take loaded bikes across the washout in high water.

Once across, we checked out the interlocking concrete blocks that had originally held the bridge decking but had been undermined by the spring melt from the glaciers hanging on the surrounding peaks. Culverts, large enough to drive a pickup truck through lay twisted and torn along the banks of the creek.

Shortly after we'd hauled our equipment across, it started raining. We ducked inside one of the culverts that had a fire-ring on the sand that had levelled the culvert's bottom. Shea dragged a couple of logs inside for us to sit on and then found a few pieces of kindling to start a fire. It was great having an energetic young person along who was ever willing to find wood and light a fire. We dug out our lunch.

Giant culverts washed away at Tuchitua River. This was as far as we could drive.

After the rain stopped, we loaded our bikes and cycled for two hours before making camp along the side of the road. There was water to drink from a nearby creek and driftwood for a fire. Although traffic wasn't a big concern, we had noticed, as we rode, fresh tire tracks made by a large machine, which we assumed had been driven by the caretaker in Tungsten. There were also plenty of bugs to chase us into our tents early in the evening.

Highway signs near the pass seem out of place.

NAHANNI THEN AND NOW

The following day dawned crystal clear. As we cooked our porridge, ate the last of our fresh fruit and drank our coffee, we began to experience the strangeness of being in an abandoned place. Just down from our campsite was a Yukon Highway maintenance sign indicating that roadwork was in progress and traffic should slow to 50 km/h. With loaded bikes, we couldn't cycle that fast even on the flat, never mind uphill. A few hours later we found a campground beside the Hyland River, complete with outhouses, fire pits and tent pads. Porcupines had moved in and eaten the sidewalls of the outhouse, making it a breezy peek show for any users. Fortunately, the porcupines had ignored the picnic table we sat on to have a power snack.

Outhouses at the campsite offered an interesting peak show.

CHAPTER 2: TO FIX A FLAT

Our next attraction was an abandoned cabin tucked in the scrub brush on the side of a hill. We walked up a trail and investigated. The unlocked cabin had food inside, a good tin roof, kindling in the wood box and a canoe stored under a tree. We knew that if we encountered trouble within the next few weeks and had to return, we'd be able to make ourselves comfortable. On the table, we found a postcard written by Matthias Schulte from Dresden, Germany, dated 1992, thanking the owners for his use of the building. He had been a Servas traveller who had stayed with my friend Joanne in Prince George before he headed north. She had advised him to wait a few weeks before heading north, as the passes would still be covered in snow. Obviously, he hadn't taken her advice.

We located the cabin on the contour map, thinking it would be great if all the dots on the maps represented such well-equipped places as this one.

Not far from the cabin was a cross, planted at the side of the road. Much later, we learned that when the mine was running and people were living in the cabin, a salesman from Watson Lake had driven along this road during a blizzard. The temperatures had fallen to minus 40°C, and his car motor stopped. The man was wearing city dress shoes and a three-piece suit. He got out of the car, thinking he could make it to the cabin, and started walking through the drifts. They found his frozen body about a week later, at the spot where the cross was erected.

Our next landmark was an old corral where horses had once been kept. There was also a small tin stove rusting in the bush, two outhouses and a few sardine cans around the firepit. The cans, we assumed, were left by hunters. But most interesting, tucked into the bush on the opposite side of the corral from the stove, was the blade of a helicopter or the wing of a small plane. It featured some lichen and moss but otherwise, being aluminum, was almost like new.

As we continued along, the road became bumpier and dotted with rocks that had bounced down from the surrounding slopes. We were leaving the Hyland River valley and starting up the pass that divides Yukon from the Northwest Territories. Soon John and I, heads down, arms straight out from the handle bars, were pushing our heavily loaded bikes up the steep hill while Shea cranked on ahead. Up and up we went, thankful to at last see Shea sitting on a rock, his bike leaning against a sign that said *Harrison Pass*. The sign declared that we were leaving Yukon, although, as we continued, we found no sign welcoming us to the Northwest Territories.

Elsebeth overlooking Mirror Lake & Kuskula Creek.

Notice warning all trespassers to go no farther.

The locked gate was obviously not meant for us.

We passed the blue-green water of beaver ponds glittering in the sun and coasted around a corner to find, on the far side of the valley, Mirror Lake, another green body of glacial melt water tucked under a red-mineralized mountain, and draining into the Flat River. The Flat is one of the major and most legendary tributaries of the Nahanni. Here, it was a mere creek that we knew would grow to a raging river by the time it reached the Nahanni. Above Mirror Lake was Kuskula Creek, surrounded by the snow-covered peaks of the Ragged Range.

The downhill from the pass became steeper, and we coasted until we saw Shea again sitting by the side of the road.

"I've got a flat."

"I've got the patching kit," I said, laying my bike down.

"Who's got the pump?"

We dug through our gear and found that we'd forgotten to pack the pump. Shea walked down the mountain, his head hanging in disappointment. We silently coasted by until we came to a junction and a small, unfinished cabin to which John immediately gravitated. Just outside the cabin I fixed a fire and put water on for tea and supper.

I hauled out the map, and my finger traced the road north toward the Flat Lakes, where we planned to camp. Then my finger swung to the south, to Tungsten. Both distances were about ten kilometers and too far to go that evening. Shea arrived just as dinner was ready, and ate ravenously. We pitched our tents, stored our gear in the cabin and slept.

The following morning, after a bowl of porridge and some strong black coffee, we cycled slowly while Shea walked, pushing his bike toward Tungsten. We came to a gate with a sign warning unauthorized persons not to enter. Those caught, the sign said, would be severely prosecuted.

"The sign isn't meant for us," I said, staring sternly at John. We argued. "There are hot springs on the far side of town," I reminded him. That perked him up. Shea caught up. I climbed under the bar of the gate. Reluctantly, John and Shea hauled their bikes through and continued along with me in the lead.

There was no sound except a raven's squawk and the distant hum of a motor. All the doors of the townsite's buildings were open and there were curtains hanging on the windows. But no kids, dogs, cars or people were seen. I felt like Marshal Dillon walking into Dodge City, where an enemy outlaw was sitting at the bar and the residents were all hiding under their beds.

At the Head Office building, we peeked inside. Behind a counter were desks still decked with coffee cups, and some typewriters had paper in them. A broom stood in one corner.

Back outside, we watched a rusted pickup truck careen around a corner and roar up the street toward us. It skidded to a stop and a smiling dark-haired man asked us what we wanted.

The main street of Tungsten with the office on the left.

Fully equipped machine shop.

"Air for the flat tire," Shea said, pointing at his bike.

Quick thinking! I thought. We weren't trespassing. We were in desperate need of help.

After introducing himself, Gerald, the man in the truck, told us we couldn't go through town alone. Company policy, he said, and invited us to throw our bikes into the back of his pickup. He then drove us to a three-bay machine shop, where we parked beside two giant yellow mining machines.

Inside the shop were pickups in each bay, surrounded by worktables and equipment. Gerald took the tire off, patched the tube and then rolled out a compressor run by a gasoline motor.

When the bike was fixed, we explained that we were going to hike north of the Flat Lakes and up Zenchuk Creek. From there, depending on how long it took, we'd go down the Rabbitkettle River and then circle back along Kuskula Creek.

"You should go for a swim in the pool before heading out."

Yes! I thought. I was starting to like Gerald, and the idea of a helpful person with a whole town full of useful equipment so close to trailhead was comforting.

We threw Shea's bike back into the truck and drove through town on the main road, past a fire station, curling rink and Gerald's house. We turned left and down a hill, passing along side a settling pond and two drainage pools.

"Pools are checked twice a year," Gerald told us. We then passed an airstrip before finally stopping beside a baseball diamond, where empty bleachers sat in the scorching sun.

"This was all built in 1961," Gerald said, flamboyantly waving his arm. "You can camp anywhere around here, any time you like," he added as we unloaded our bikes.

The Tungsten Hot Springs fed by 13 contributing streams.

"We've got stuff at the junction," I said. "But maybe after our hike."

"After you have a soak, come back to the house. It's the only house with lights on and doors open."

"Yes, you pointed it out to us," I reminded him.

He drove off, tires tearing at the gravel, and we turned to check out the hot spring. A fungus-infested outdoor pool complete with diving board and a lifesaving ring was what we saw first. Nearby were shop-made, outdoor barbeque pits packed with the remains of numerous festivities that must have taken place long before. Then, tucked in the shadow of the mountain, we saw a tiny A-frame.

Inside we found a steaming pool encased with wood, the bottom lined with pea gravel and dotted with large rocks on which we could sit. Towels and suits hung on hooks in the foyer and dozens of shampoo bottles and bars of soap adorned the bottom plate of the pool's frame. We kicked off our boots and jumped in.

Tungsten as seen from the plane.

CHAPTER 2: TO FIX A FLAT

After luxuriating in the hot pool for an hour, we cycled back to Gerald's house and met up with Terri Pitt, Gerald's wife, and their two kids, Natasha and Alex. We scarfed down some homemade muffins and coffee, watched Natasha chase Alex with a stick and then loaded our bikes on the truck and went on a tour of the town with Gerald.

Gerald Pitt. Photo first published in the Prince George Citizen in 1994.

We first drove around the house, past the school, the medical center and then up to the next level, where the apartment buildings sat. The first building we went into contained the single men's rooms. Each had a plush carpet, private bathroom with glassed-in shower, a built-in dresser, a desk and a telephone. The second building was the married quarters that had one-, two- or three-bedroom suites with picture windows overlooking the Ragged Range. Each apartment was equipped with a washer, dryer and dishwasher. The entire place was upscale.

"That's the mill," Gerald said pointing to a huge metal building on the level beneath us. "I never go in there. It's a rust gob."

Tungsten mill site.

Gerald then took us into the underground tunnel along a two-lane paved road that, according to him, went up into the mountain at a 3 percent grade. This allowed the water seeping from the rock to drain out the shaft. At the end of the one-kilometer tunnel were a fully equipped machine shop and a huge ventilation fan that sucked up the bad air. Bolts holding heavy pieces of steel across fractures secured the mineshaft and the entire passageway was encased in a metal mesh stocking to prevent injury from falling rock. Gerald said the mine had a great safety record.

We exited the mineshaft and, as we climbed onto our bikes, we promised to return in a week or two, after we'd explored farther north.

"You'll find three empty cabins at the south end of the Flat Lakes," Gerald said. "You can use any of them. There's also the conservation officer's cottage on the other side of the creek. You'll see it."

"Funny story connected to that one," he added as he climbed into his truck.

Gerald told us that the conservation officer's name was Stan Bors; he had come from Poland about ten years before and he had a German shepherd dog called Foot who followed him everywhere. During the summer Stan spent a lot of time fishing and often brought fresh fish to the house, which Terry would cook.

"Last autumn, Stan became so paranoid he imagined he was being ambushed by Indians," Gerald continued. "In his panic he shot and grazed himself in the leg, but he was able to get into the cabin and radio-phone me. I called the cops in Watson Lake. They sent out the SWAT team."

Gerald laughed and explained that they found no one, and eventually Stan admitted to faking the whole event.

"Poor guy," I said. "I guess some of the stories about the Nahanni got to him."

"See you later, Gerald," John said. "If you don't see us in a month, call in the SWAT team!"

"It won't be a fake report!"

We waved and cycled off.

It took the rest of the day to collect our stored gear at the junction and pedal to the Flat Lakes. Just as the end of the lake appeared, we found Stan's cabin off the road on the east side of a small creek and a field of poppies. The door was locked and the plywood welcome mat had dozens of spikes sticking up through the wood. The road cut to the left around the bottom of the lake and up a hill. At the top was a well-marked path, which we followed to an abandoned cabin with a front porch that featured a store-bought bench. The door had a clasp but wasn't locked, and it opened into the bedroom.

This became our home at the Flat Lakes.

Inside, we each claimed a bunk and then snooped around. The cabin was fully stocked with dishes and pots, bedding and even a bit of dry food sealed in glass containers. I placed the previous occupant's slippers into the cupboard and John got a piece of wire from the shed to secure the stovepipe. We ate at the picnic table by the beach overlooking the lake and hit the soft beds inside, early.

"It's weird being in a stranger's bed," John said. "His slippers by the door, dishes in the drying rack."

CHAPTER 3

HISTORY OF THE FLAT LAKES

Materials pertinent to the history of the Flat Lakes are almost nonexistent. Over the years, we put the history together from books such as *Nahanni* by Dick Turner, *Nahanni Revisited* by Al Lewis, *Pilots of the Purple Twilight* by Philip H. Godsell, and *Flight of the Red Beaver* by Larry Whitesitt. We also ordered, through the park service, a thick wad of interviews done by W. D. Addison with any old Nahanni trappers and prospectors still alive in 1975/76. One interview was sealed until 2010, which we eventually got. Finally, Sherry Bradford, daughter of George Dalziel, a key figure in any Nahanni history, let us read, in part, a manuscript written by him.

The first whites at the lake and along the river were trappers and prospectors such as Poole Field. In 1910 a Norwegian, Martin Jorgenson, left his post at Ross River in Yukon, located just west of the upper Nahanni, and came across the divide to prospect. He sent a letter out to his friend, Poole Field, saying that he'd found gold on the Flat River. Field went to the mouth of the Flat and found Jorgenson's cabin burned and his skeleton not far from the cabin. Coming from Ross River, Jorgenson had to have passed the Flat Lakes on the way to the Flat River.

The most realistic gold seekers who arrived next were trappers rather than prospectors: George Dalziel, Bill Cormack and Nazar Zenchuk.

We've put together a broad history of the Nahanni and Liard watersheds from our research materials, along with any RCMP reports we could find. But the contradictions are endless—these authors and interviewees were writing or talking of times long ago.

I'm giving you the parts pertaining to the Flat Lakes without noting the contradictions. I will try to explain those contradictions at the end of this section.

GEORGE DALZIEL

Most of the permanent white inhabitants of the area came in the late '20s and '30s, based themselves in Fort Simpson and trapped along the Liard River. Most were young men driven off farms and away from families by the Depression. Word was that there was good money in trapping. And there were also rumours of gold.

The arrival of these men made trouble for the First Nations people in the Liard River country and the whites who managed these peoples' lives. As the RCMP describe it, the Flat River watershed was trapped and hunted by the Liard Band, who moved through the winter to various camps and then, to trade, came down to Nahanni Butte or Fort Simpson on skin boats once the waterways were free of ice. Patterson describes his encounters with them, trading tea for moose meat.

Grant McConachie and George Dalziel with their mechanic. The Curtis Robin in the background was purchased by Dal in 1936. Photo was reproduced with permission from Bernie Richardson at the Aviation Museum of Alberta.

George Dalziel turned into the biggest trouble for the Aboriginal people and therefore the police, too. But Dalziel was a bit different than the usual greenhorn farmer's kid. He was well educated and had listened to stories about life in the north.

He was born in Vancouver in 1908 and went to St George's Private School. During those years, Dalziel was a boy scout and learned to trap from his troop leader, Reverend Sykes. Dalziel's trapline ran along the North Shore Mountains from Point Atkinson to Horseshoe Bay. When he became a troop leader, he in turn, shared his skills with Ian McTaggart Cowan. Cowan became a biologist; his brother Patrick was a meteorologist who became the first president of Simon Fraser University. This information comes from Ian McTaggart Cowan's biography.

By 1923 Dalziel had hopes of becoming a medical doctor, but a story in the newspaper changed his mind, and his life. The story was about a

CHAPTER 3: HISTORY OF THE FLAT LAKES

trapper and his daughter who trapped one winter along the Liard and then tried to paddle their boat loaded with furs through Devil's Canyon on the B.C. stretch of the river. When their boat was swept away in the raging spring runoff, the father died. But the daughter survived and managed to make it to Fort Simpson, located at the confluence of the Liard and Mackenzie Rivers in the Northwest Territories, with the furs intact.

A year after reading that story, Dalziel was accepted at Vancouver College to study medicine. A few months later, he went home for dinner and met an interesting guest, an RCMP inspector who regaled the family with tales of trappers living on a wild, salmon-filled river that zigzags through B.C. and Yukon. And as it turned out, it was the same river that had taken the life of the trapper Dalziel had previously read about. The inspector talked extensively about unskilled white men trying to live in the north, men who weren't prepared to hunt for food and thus starved to death. And those who did survive the trapping season over the winter often died in the rough spring waters, trying to get their furs to market.

Dalziel went back to his studies, but the stories haunted him. Then, close to final exams, he found that his father had made some bad investments and couldn't afford to pay for the coming year's tuition. With this problem tucked into the back of his mind, he went to a lecture by a guest speaker and, at the end of the talk, asked the professor how much money he made from one such lecture. The instructor told him, "Five dollars, and I have to provide my own skeleton."

At that time a marten skin was worth around $50, a fisher about $30, and restrictions on trapping were almost nonexistent. Dalziel knew this. When he was a boy scout he had learned how to trap along the streams of North Vancouver and felt he had some skills to challenge the harsh environment he was hearing so much about.

Dalziel made up his mind. In the spring of 1926, when he was 18 years old and had one year of medical training behind him, he booked his boat passage to Wrangell, Alaska. He had a hundred dollars in his pocket that he'd borrowed from his mother and another $29 he'd saved from his trapping excursions in Vancouver. His companion was a dog called Mutt. On the boat, Dalziel met Ray Bowers, a Californian who had just finished his medical residency in Vancouver and wanted a year's vacation. They both had rifles and ammunition and planned on living off the land for the following year. They became a team.

From Wrangell they headed up the Stikine River to Telegraph Creek. Along the way they saw their first grizzly, first moose and first wolf. They were thrilled. In Telegraph Creek they hired the Morrison brothers, the only ones in the region who had a motorized vehicle, to transport their thousand pounds of gear over the mountains to Dease Lake. The cost was 20 cents a pound for the freight, but that didn't include them. To save money, they walked behind the truck.

To help with the food supply, Dalziel shot a moose, which earned him the respect of the Morrison brothers and made Mutt appreciate his new life in the north. The group made it to Dease Lake with no mishaps. After building a boat, Bowers and Dalziel worked their way across the lake and down the Dease River to Lower Post on the Liard River. On the way they shot their first mink. At Lower Post, Dalziel cashed the fur in for the monumental sum of $20.

The two men continued down the Liard, passing through the 40-mile canyon with little problem. At Porcupine Bar they pulled in and found a cabin where Oscar Anderson, a local prospector and miner, had trapped 200 lynx the previous year. As proof of the story, the skulls were found strewn around the cabin. This confirmed to Dalziel that there was a lot more money to be made in trapping than in lecturing or doctoring.

Once they reached Cranberry Rapids on the Liard, they got into trouble, as the rapids were long and the water was high. Luckily, they'd been smart enough to leave some of their gear on shore while they tried running the rapids. They ended in the drink but managed to haul the overturned boat to the south shore and save their rifles and an axe. But sadly, some of their food, most of their bedding and almost all of their traps were gone.

They looked around and liked the spot at the confluence of a small river, the Rabbit, just downstream from where they hit shore. It looked like good trapping country, so they started building a cabin. Once the walls were up and they had carved new paddles, they floated down river about a mile in the course of crossing back to the north side. They dragged their canoe upriver to a spot above their camp on the opposite side, and walked up to collect the rest of their gear.

Dalziel was exhilarated by his near-death experience, but the event demoralized Bowers, who returned by foot to Lower Post. Dalziel never saw or heard from him again. Nor did anyone else. In historical records, Bowers is the first of many missing persons attached to Dalziel's name.

Dalziel continued alone back down to the Rabbit River, where he finished building the cabin that he and Bowers had started. He spent the winter trapping with the few traps he had left. It was during this first summer and winter in the Liard area that he learned the important skills of survival, and he attributed his success to observing both the Indigenous people and the animals and adapting their survival skills to himself. He ate a lot of fat. He kept himself dry. He kept his matches dry. He used dogs to carry gear and for food, but only when he had to. He eventually became the best "stick man" in the north.

Dalziel and his dog Mutt stayed on the Rabbit River for the following winter. Once, while they were on Fishing Lake at the top end of his trap line, wolves surrounded them. He tied Mutt to a tree and, with pistol in hand, climbed the tree to safety. The wolves barked and howled and Dalziel fired, but in that cold, the bullets didn't have much power and couldn't penetrate the heavy animal fur. Then Dalziel made a mistake. He slipped off the branch he was standing on and dropped his gun. The wolves saw this, grabbed Mutt by the hind legs and dragged him into the middle of the pack. But after they killed Mutt, the wolves lost interest in Dalziel and moved on down the lake. This event developed in Dalziel hatred for wolves that lasted the rest of his life.

By 1934, after eight years of trapping along the Liard, Dalziel's survival skills were the envy of his co-trappers. He had, over the years, been able to successfully work 200 miles of challenging trap line located in the sparsely populated wilds of the Yukon/Northwest Territories.

In late summer of 1934, to test himself, or maybe because he wanted a challenge, he travelled overland from Lower Post to Fort Norman on the Mackenzie River, a distance of 600 miles (950 km). Walking about 15 miles (25 km) a day, he crossed some of the most rugged country in Canada, the mysterious Nahanni, said to be spooked by missing gold seekers (the McLeod brothers, found headless and tied to trees in what came to be known as Deadman Valley) and patrolled by the Naha First Nation people, who were rumoured to be head-hunters and led by a female chief with snow-white hair. Dalziel, like Patterson, scoffed at these stories.

On his journey, Dalziel stopped only once—for a two-day rest. He carried a hunting rifle and was accompanied by a few pack dogs that carried and ate most of the meat he shot, plus his Hudson's Bay blanket that he used for his bed. His only luxury was a small sack of tea leaves for his nightly drink.

His route went north up the Coal River and over the territorial divide to McMillan Lake, where he stayed a night with Gus Kraus, Bill Clark and Jack Stanier, old Nahanni heroes who were digging holes along McLeod Creek and running gravel through sluice boxes. He'd met them before and found their stories and their fascination with gold amusing if not stupid.

As did Raymond Patterson, who started his book *Dangerous River* with an account of the McLeod find—"A story that rivals anything that even Jack London's fertile imagination could bring forth."

Dick North describes the Nahanni gold rush as starting in 1933 with Stanier and Clark, who flew into McMillan Lake and came back with three ounces of gold. Patterson called that "an episode of romantic buffoonery."

Viv looking for gold on an unnamed creek that flows into the South Nahanni River. Photo by Joanne Armstrong.

As Dalziel moved northeast, he built small rafts with which to cross any open rivers and followed game trails through scrub brush whenever possible. Once he reached the Flat River and its tributaries, he cut across land to the Rabbitkettle River through Hole-in-the-Wall valley. Faille's preferred route through was up Irvine Creek, which drains Hole-in-the-Wall into the Flat. In Hole-in-the-Wall valley, Dalziel saw a high mountain, recently determined to be the highest in the Northwest Territories. The mountain had a cliff face that would eventually attract recreational climbers who had the wherewithal to rent float planes.

From the confluence of the Rabbitkettle River and Hole-in-the-Wall Creek, Dalziel followed the Rabbitkettle River to the hot springs. At the confluence of the Rabbitkettle and the Nahanni he again built a raft and crossed the wide and swift river. He then followed game trails to Raft Creek and up Raft to Black Wolf Creek. At Black Wolf Creek the weather turned bad, with rain and sleet, so he camped just a little way up the creek at Grizzly Lake for a few days, to rest himself and his dogs. Beyond Grizzly

Lake, the landscape became rougher, and at one point he had to lower the dogs by rope, one at a time, down a cliff face to get beyond that set of mountains. I'm not sure how he did this or if it is even possible, but the story is in every tale about Dalziel's epic trip.

As he travelled, he found old stone axe cuttings and signs of Indigenous camps. By then he was almost at his desired destination of Fort Norman. He passed the South Redstone River, Dall Lake (named after the sheep) and the Dahadinni River, and finally came to the Mackenzie River. In this section of the hike, he saw more abandoned Indigenous campsites with artifacts and tepee-pole holes. He also found that some of the camps had gravesites where whole families had been buried, possibly having died of smallpox.

Dalziel rafted the Mackenzie, and forty-two days and 600 miles after starting, he landed in Fort Norman. After cleaning up and devouring a home-cooked meal at the hotel, he won a shooting contest with Wop May, the prize being a plane ride to Edmonton. May was one of Canada's best known WWI fighter pilots, famous for his battles with the Red Baron and for his recent efforts, two years earlier, in hunting down Albert Johnson, the Mad Trapper.

Through the winter of 1934-35 Dalziel trapped in the Root River area, half way between Fort Norman and Nahanni Butte, where he caught 130 prime furs. He hired Wop May to fly him and his furs out to Edmonton so he could get a better price than he could at Fort Simpson. News of the winter's haul, $7,000 in value, hit the newspapers.

With the encouragement of Wop May, Dalziel booked into flying lessons with Moss Burbidge, another retired RAF pilot. It took just two weeks before Dalziel's daredevil personality surfaced, and he did a few tailspins in the plane. These turns pulled the guy-wires so tight they almost broke. He was expelled from flying school. The price of repairing the plane after this escapade made the profits of his winter's haul drop noticeably. Regardless of being a hellion, he eventually got his licence and immediately purchased his first plane, a Curtis Robin, licensed

CF-ALZ. The plane had been owned by Grant McConachie, ultimately the first president of Canadian Pacific Airlines.

Dalziel's plane at Glacier Lake. Photo donated by Sherry Bradford.

Dalziel then went into the flying business, but not as an ordinary bush pilot. Combining his old passion with the new one, he became the first flying trapper. The rules at the time were that a licensed trapper could have assistants. Dalziel established trap lines in out-of-the-way places that had not been trapped before and hired his first assistants, greenhorns from the prairies, George and Bill Cormack.

Dalziel's career as flying trapper was short, a couple of years at the most. He was legislated out of business by an act of Parliament in February 1937.

The government didn't like him using the less expensive Yukon licence and didn't like him infringing on traditional Aboriginal trapping areas.

GEORGE & BILL CORMACK

The following information was taken from tapes made presumably by Addison (interviewer's name is not on the tape) on March 17, 1979, at Bill Cormack's home in North Vancouver.

During the Depression, Bill Cormack and his brother George, rookies fresh off the Saskatchewan prairies, headed north on a freight train, hoping to land a job when they arrived in Lac La Biche. It was 1932. Even though they had a hundred bucks in their pocket, the police suspected the brothers were vagrants. Rather than cause trouble, they bought tickets going even farther north, to Fort Smith. After a year of working in the area (late 1933) they reached Fort Simpson. Dalziel had had a winter of trapping on the Rabbit River and was recruiting potential trapping partners.

There is a one-year discrepancy between the dates that Bill Cormack gave Addison and the date that Dalziel purchased his plane. Dalziel bought his plane in 1935, and this date can be verified in the Edmonton Aviation Museum's records, whereas Cormack claims he arrived in Fort Simpson in late winter of 1934 and met Dalziel, who already had his plane. Cormack's date is quoted from memory and after a forty-year lapse. So, it was certainly the winter of 1935-1936, specifically January 2, 1936, that Dalziel flew Cormack into the Flat Lakes.

This came about when Dalziel saw the Cormack brothers in Fort Simpson and made an offer. He would fly Bill into the Flat Lakes, show him how to trap, and pick him up in the spring. Brother George would be stationed on the Rabbitkettle River with the same training. Dalziel told the brothers that an experienced trapper named Nazar Zenchuk would be working around the Skinboat Lakes, about 30 miles south of the Flat Lakes. George's line, on the Rabbitkettle, was downriver from Skinboat Lakes. Cormack says you could manage about 20 miles a day in spring when the going was hard, so each man would be just a few days walking distance from the other.

The deal was that Bill and George would buy the traps and then Dalziel would fly them in and out at no cost upfront, but they would split the winter's haul by thirds—one for the trapper, one for Dalziel and one for the plane. It sounded good to the Cormacks, so they agreed. They also needed trapping licences. At that time the cost of a trapping licence in the Northwest Territories was a prohibitive $100, but men could purchase a Yukon license for $5. No wonder the Fort Simpson authorities were upset with Dalziel.

When Bill landed at the Flat Lakes, the temperature was minus 60° F. It was silent and intimidating. Dalziel stayed five days, showing Bill how to strike a tent and build a fire so he'd be warm all night, how to set traps above the timber line, where the animals wintered, and what to do with the animals once caught. This entire process is described in detail by Al Lewis in *Nahanni Remembered*. Lewis trapped for Dalziel near the Rabbitkettle in 1937. As Lewis tells it, Dalziel gave his trappers a thorough course, but mainly in trapping, skinning and preparing marten and beaver. He also helped them set up Siwash camps with stocks of firewood leaning against trees, at their turn-around points.

Dalziel did the same with George on the Rabbitkettle River. Zenchuk, of course, was experienced and needed no guidance, just the flight in.

Cormack reports that Dalziel always used tents, although it is known that Zenchuk eventually had a cabin at the confluence of the Caribou and Flat Rivers. Lewis reports that a few years after the Cormacks trapped on the Flat/Rabbitkettle, the last of Dalziel's assistant trappers, Harry Vandaele, asked about this. Dalziel told Vandaele he thought cabins unsafe; they always burned down.

A cache, however, was essential. Only they were animal-proof. Every trapper had stories about how animals got into cabins when they could smell food and skins inside. They often told the story of Faille's cabin being invaded by a wolverine that ripped off the chimney to make an accessible escape hole in the roof.

John Harris shares a scotch and many tales with Al Lewis, author of Nahanni Remembered.

Dalziel's specialty was a two-pole cache—two poles nailed or tied between two fat trees, the trees topped, poles corduroyed across the poles connecting the two trees, and stovepipes nailed around the trees so animals couldn't climb up. Dalziel would have helped the Cormacks make one of these at each camp.

During Cormack's first winter, Dalziel popped back and forth between the two brothers and Zenchuk about once a month, bringing in more food or any other supplies the men needed, and also checking to make certain the men were safe, and picking up pelts. These he was known to fly to Edmonton, where they fetched a better price than at Nahanni Butte or Fort Simpson. It didn't take much time for him to acquire a full planeload.

During one visit with Bill, Dalziel was revving up his motor and made a bet that Bill would catch at least 200 marten over the winter. Bill expressed some doubt, but took the bet anyway. Marten at that time were selling for $38 a skin, and 200 would result in a take of about $7,500, ten times what the average farmer was making. The prize of the bet was a case of champagne. That spring, Bill cashed in 212 furs and Dalziel, after collecting his case, shared one of the bottles.

Bill Cormack, who later became a pilot, was impressed by Dalziel's abilities as a flier and as a trapper. About Dalziel, he said, "He knew the country well. He could judge how deep the snow was, and the direction of the wind."

According to Cormack, he returned again in the fall to trap for another winter, but his dates don't fit with other recorded dates and this is important to the mystery surrounding Dalziel. It most likely was late that spring (1936) when things got a bit strange. The occasion became one of the big Nahanni mysteries after the deaths of the McLeod brothers—the disappearance of Joe Mulholland and Bill Eppler.

In March 1936, Dalziel flew supplies into Bennett Creek, where Gus Kraus and Bill Clark were prospecting, and he told them that he had dropped Eppler and Mulholland off at Glacier Lake during the latter part of February. After leaving Kraus and Clark, Dalziel flew into the Flat Lakes and also told Cormack that Eppler and Mulholland were at Glacier Lake. Mulholland and Eppler were buying the flight only, as Eppler was an experienced, licensed trapper and Mulholland his assistant. They would trap until the ice moved out of the upper Nahanni in May or early June and then float their catch out in skin boats.

Cormack says that when Mulholland and Eppler didn't show up (it was in mid-May, according to the RCMP report) concerns were raised at Nahanni Butte. Dalziel and a police officer flew to Glacier Lake and everything looked normal. This is confirmed in a police report. Dalziel then picked up Cormack and they flew to the lake. They found that Eppler and Mulholland "had picked up their traps off the trap line and were coming out on the first open water. Their cabin was not burned." Cormack confirmed that the traps were in the cache and everything looked normal. Cormack thought that the two had headed out on foot.

But when he looked for signs on the creek that flowed out of Glacier Lake and into the Nahanni, he saw no indication that the men had gone that way; no tracks, no fire rings, no disturbance of the early spring vegetation.

According to Al Lewis, Vandaele flew in with Dalziel on the search and reported to Truesdell and the RCMP that they had searched the cabin. Later, Vandaele told Lewis that Dalziel hadn't flown him into any lake.

Harry Vandaele in the back row, on the right. His brother is in the front row, 3rd from the left. Photo donated by Al Lewis.

Dalziel took Cormack back to the Flat Lakes. He should have reappeared a couple of weeks later, but he didn't. While waiting, Bill ran out of grub so he walked down the Flat to Zenchuk's cabin on the Caribou River, and together they agreed to walk out to Nahanni Butte before the snow pack melted, picking up George on the Rabbitkettle along the way.

CHAPTER 3: HISTORY OF THE FLAT LAKES

It was a tough trip for the Cormacks, and when they got to Nahanni Butte, much to their surprise, Dalziel was there. Always quick with an answer, Dalziel told the three men that he had been looking after some other trappers. But the likelihood was that he'd had his plane impounded by the police.

Dalziel then flew Bill Cormack back to the Flat Lakes, but Bill refused to make a deal with Dalziel for the following winter. Being left behind once was more than enough. He told Dalziel that Wop May would pick him up in the spring.

NAZAR ZENCHUK

The main feeder creek of the Flat Lakes is Zenchuk Creek. It is easy to find out from official records who or what various features were named for, but in the cases of the "who" there is often no explanation of the "why."

The first known map of the Nahanni River watershed below Virginia Falls was made by Willie McLeod. It marked the site of the gold find and the location where the remains of his brothers were found. This was later called Deadmen Valley. In 1916, Corporal David Churchill, Fort Simpson Detachment, drew "the earliest rough sketch of the Nahanni River." Patterson made the map, exhibited in his book, that was used before and during the "episode of romantic buffoonery" in 1933–1935. None of these maps goes as far west as the Flat Lakes.

Some features of the landscape were named by Dalziel; Gus Kraus mentions Hole-in-the-Wall Lake, Sunblood Mountain, Stonemarten Lake, Flood Creek and Skull Creek in this regard. Dalziel might have tagged Zenchuk Creek with his most faithful partner's name. But there is no indication that Dalziel ever took Zenchuk there to trap.

Nazar Zenchuk in 1928. Photo donated by Sherry Bradford, Dal's daughter.

Information on Nazar Zenchuk is available in an interview of him, done for the parks service by W.D. Addison. The interview was taped and typed. The typist, not understanding much of what Zenchuk said, pretty much produced a phonetic transcript. Dalziel, for example, becomes Daryl Seal. The interviewer didn't ask for much clarity, so the interview leaves many questions unanswered and dates inconsistent. It is, however, the main source of information on Zenchuk for the time before he arrives on the Liard River. After that, he is mentioned often by Turner in his book and others in the Addison interviews. Usually, he is connected to Dalziel.

Nazar Zenchuk was born in Kiev, Ukraine, on December 14, 1896, to Platal Zenchuk (or Zinchuk) and Orel Packla. Nazar joined the Russian army in 1916 and was wounded in 1917. After he recovered, he became a policeman and for the next six years worked in Moscow. During that time, he married a Russian woman, and they moved to Poland.

Things were tough in Eastern Europe at that time, so Zenchuk and his wife agreed that he'd come to Canada, a country he'd read a lot about. He'd make a bundle of money and then send for his wife and parents. He doesn't

CHAPTER 3: HISTORY OF THE FLAT LAKES

mention having any children. He arrived in Melrose, Saskatchewan, on August 15, 1928, in time to work as a farm hand for the harvesting season. That fall he left for Edmonton, where he got a job making railway ties for 75 cents an hour, a good wage at that time, Zenchuk claims.

When that job was complete, Zenchuk paid a conductor $20 for the privilege of riding in a boxcar heading to Winnipeg. However, within a few hours of departure, the police hauled him off and sent him on his way. That was his first experience of being cheated by a Canadian.

He then hitched a ride over to Cochrane and worked for the highways department for $17-$18 a day, a salary that was much higher than that paid by the railway.

By 1930, Zenchuk was back in Edmonton living at a Chinese boarding house on 104th Street, where he had a cubical room with shared bathroom and paid $1 a day for meals. The stock market had crashed, and jobs were scarce. Zenchuk and a fellow Ukrainian bought the boarding house and started a restaurant of sorts, charging customers 25 cents a meal regardless of whether the customer lived in the house or not. During the early 1930s, 25 loaves of bread sold for a dollar, a dozen eggs went for two-bits and a pound of lard cost about 15 cents, so Zenchuk was able to do a bit better than break even.

By 1932, the Depression had left millions unemployed and hungry and the relief lines long. An Edmonton health inspector felt he had to do something about the long lines at the food kitchens. Wielding a knife in one hand and poking his finger at Zenchuk's chest with the other, he convinced Zenchuk to feed people on relief. The inspector claimed the government would pay him 25 cents for each person who was fed two meals a day. I suspect the government actually paid more, but the inspector needed his own pieces of government silver, so, knowing he was dealing with an illiterate immigrant, he took about half. The Zenchuk/Addison interview isn't clear about this, but as best I can guess, this was Zenchuk's second experience with a not-so-honest Canadian.

Soon after setting up the food kitchen, something happened between Zenchuk's partner and the police, so the two left Edmonton. On these events, there is no clarity in the interview. I assume Zenchuk had someone look after the house for him, because at a later date, he mentions being at the house again. In the transcript the friend's name is "Awareco," which sounds like a bastardization of a nickname the locals may have given him. There is no other information available about this friend.

After leaving Edmonton, Zenchuk wanted to reach Yellowknife, Bear Lake and the Liard River, places he had heard about. He and his newfound partner and fellow Slav, John Lomar, boated up the Liard with the intention of trapping that winter on or near the Nahanni River. Here, the Zenchuk interview can be correlated with official records kept by the Northwest Territories authorities, other interviews done by Addison with locals, Turner's *Nahanni* and my own interview with Sherry Bradford, Dalziel's daughter, who knew Zenchuk and was very fond of him.

When Lomar and Zenchuk arrived at Nahanni Butte, presumably in late summer of 1932, they were told that the Nahanni River was far too dangerous a place to spend the winter. The tales were so vivid that Lomar and Zenchuk took the advice of the old-timers and headed over to the Toad River, closer to Fort Nelson.

In the fall, Zenchuk met Dalziel somewhere near Fort Nelson. They struck up a conversation and Dalziel told Zenchuk what he'd need to survive a winter trapping in the north. Zenchuk took his advice.

After spending the winter of 1932-33 at the mouth of the Toad where it reaches the Liard, Zenchuk and Lomar walked out to Fort Nelson in April, a distance of 100 miles (160 km) hauling their winter's catch with them. In Fort Nelson, someone impersonating a police officer stamped Zenchuk's furs and gave him a ticket. He argued, saying he wanted cash. A disagreement ensued and the police from Fort Simpson were called in. After talking to the police, Zenchuk retrieved his sack of furs, only to discover that most of his valuable furs had been replaced with flour. He ended up trading the remaining furs at Northern Traders in Fort Liard for a few hundred dollars. Zenchuk had again been cheated.

Ollie Rollog, shows off the Nahanni dress code. Photo by Norm Thomas taken in 1952, and donated by H. Martyn.

That summer, Zenchuk went to Little Bear River, a tributary to the Mackenzie River just south of Norman Wells, and built two boats to haul goods for officials and trappers across the rapids. He accumulated a few dollars and went to Yellowknife, where he met up with Father Goulet, who performed a marriage ceremony for Zenchuk and an Indigenous lady. Undoubtedly Goulet wasn't told about the Russian wife. On September 27, 1933, Zenchuk started building a cabin for Father Goulet.

But for the winter he wanted to trap in the Nahanni region with his new wife. Before he finished Goulet's cabin, he went to Fort Simpson to purchase a trapper's licence. The police inspector demanded $100. Zenchuk argued as best he could in his broken English that the licence should cost $5, like it had in Toad River, but the inspector insisted. Zenchuk didn't have $100, since he'd been cheated in Fort Nelson, so the inspector said he could pay for the licence in the spring with the money he'd earn from trapping all winter. Zenchuk and his wife went up the Flat River to Skinboat Lakes and trapped for the winter.

They had lots of neighbours, whether they wanted them or not. Earlier that year, Jack Stanier and Poole Field had obtained a map that was supposed to indicate the locations of the gold the famous, albeit dead, McLeod bothers had found. Stanier and Field had flown into McLeod Creek, not far from Skinboat Lakes, and then out to Fort Simpson to form a syndicate of financiers who would help raise money for prospecting.

Zenchuk's winter catch was good, and when he returned to Nahanni Butte on May 7, 1934 he had about $7,000 worth of furs. Bill Eppler and Jack Mulholland, who ran the post at Nahanni Butte, confiscated the furs, saying Zenchuk didn't have a licence. Zenchuk complained to the police, and the case ended in court. Eppler got Mulholland, Gus Kraus and Bill Clark to testify against Zenchuk before Magistrate Truesdell, who was also a good friend of Kraus and Clark. The case resulted in Zenchuk losing his furs, but he was awarded $200 and some grub for the following winter. At this point, Canadians weren't looking too honest to Zenchuk.

In his interview, Zenchuk is confused about what he did that summer and following winter. One story says he left to prospect on the Firth River with Poole Field, where he made six claims but found no gold. The other story says he went up to Herschel Island, where Field supposedly found gold nuggets five times the size of his pills.

That winter, Stanier and Field returned to McLeod Creek numerous times, and in early 1934 they found some old sluice boxes believed to have belonged to the McLeod brothers. But no matter how much they prospected, the rich gold veins eluded them.

It was a year after the court case that Zenchuk regained contact with George Dalziel, who was also not the best friend of Truesdell or the RCMP officer in Fort Simpson. Dalziel sympathized with Zenchuk for being cheated. Once Dalziel purchased his plane, he flew Zenchuk to the Caribou

River, a tributary of the Flat. They purchased Yukon trapping licences and planned to claim that all their furs came from the Yukon side of the border. Zenchuk spent the winter of 1935-36 trapping for Dalziel, and his nearest neighbours were the Cormack brothers.

Gus Kraus near the Nahanni River. Photo donated by D. R. Flook.

During that winter John Lomar, Zenchuk's friend, was on the La Biche River and had a date to meet Zenchuk at his cabin near the mouth of the Caribou for Christmas. But John didn't show. However, the La Biche is a tributary to the Athabasca River, a long way from the Flat, so it seems Zenchuk was misremembering or not being understood by the interviewer.

According to Gus Kraus, Zenchuk and Lomar left their cabin at the mouth of the Caribou and walked up the Flat to Faille's cabin near Irvine Creek. At the same time, Kraus, Bill Clark, and Harry Vandaele and Milt Campbell, all having spent a futile winter trying to find the McLeod strike, were coming down the Flat to Faille's cabin. They met there and found Faille had a bucket of beans and a couple of dead moose, which they devoured. Zenchuk still had a sack of flour in his cache at the Caribou, and they decided to follow the break-up down there to get it.

Zenchuk says that Lomar disappeared around this time, though no one else mentions that. After he disappeared, the suspicion of foul play lay on Zenchuk's shoulders. The police questioned him, but nothing was proven. A year or so later, Zenchuk learned that his friend had fallen into the river while the ice was running, got very cold and subsequently caught pneumonia and died.

There is no official record anywhere else about this, though it is also true that Lomar's name disappears from the Nahanni histories. What really happened on that float out was a continuing search for Mulholland and Eppler. Faille believed that the two men would follow the ice out of the upper Nahanni for a ways or walk overland, hauling their furs down Irvine Creek.

On the way out, the men found cuttings and camps in various places, but nothing conclusive. The whole bunch of trappers and prospectors made it out safely in the spring of 1936, except for Mulholland and Eppler and Lomar was never mentioned again.

CHAPTER 4

DISCREPANCIES OF THE FLAT LAKE TRAPPERS

By late spring of 1936, there were three men missing: Eppler and Mulholland, and Lomar. The story is riddled with discrepancies.

The Flat Lakes was first trapped, according to Dalziel, by him and a fellow named George Taylor. But Bill Cormack's 1975 interview with Addison has Cormack being the first to share a trap line with Dalziel on the Flat Lakes in 1936.

During the winter of 1935-36, Albert Faille was on Irvine Creek. The Campbell bothers were on McLeod Creek, looking for gold, and on their way out for the summer they met Clark at Faille's cabin. Faille told them that Eppler and Mulholland had not walked out by way of Irvine Creek with their winter supply of furs that they had trapped at either Glacier Lake or Rabbitkettle Lake.

The RCMP has no record of Lomar disappearing. Addison's interview just says that in 1935-36, Zenchuk and Lomar trapped together on the Caribou River and came out with Kraus and Clark. There is no mention of the Cormack brothers.

With no mention of Lomar, Cormack says that after he, brother George and Zenchuk walked out, they arrived at Nahanni Butte and found Dalziel there. Dalziel told them he was late picking them up because he had others to look after. More likely, the police had taken his plane. It was definitely impounded for a time during the summer of 1936, because it took a "miner's meeting," described by Kraus, to convince Judge Truesdell to release the plane so a further search could be made for Eppler and Mulholland.

Lewis was of the opinion that the plane was in hock because Dalziel was always shooting wolves, which "he hated with a vengeance." Turner says that it was because of trapping violations. He said Dalziel had a bad attitude to officialdom, an attitude that Turner shared. Turner felt that the officials were there to keep whites out and turn the Northwest Territories into a vast native reserve. That was why you paid so much for a permit, he thought, and why you weren't allowed to take beaver most years, whereas the Aboriginals could. Dalziel alludes in his manuscript to a conflict in the spring of 1936 over some marten he trapped live for someone who wanted to breed them; as with Zenchuk, he'd been promised the permit when he brought them in. He may have had his plane impounded while the police sorted this issue out.

According to Dalziel, in February 1936, he flew Eppler and Mulholland into Glacier Lake. Turner has it at Christmastime, and Lewis makes it January. Dalziel later reported to police that he thought the two were experienced "stick men," but found out later they weren't. Everyone else says Eppler was experienced, but the RCMP say he was foolhardy. Turner partly agrees, saying Eppler was often impatient and was afraid of nothing.

Dalziel fishing at Glacier Lake. Photo donated by Sherry Bradford.

Turner says that it was Rabbitkettle Lake, not Glacier Lake, where the men trapped. He says Eppler decided to move on because his line near Nahanni Butte wasn't producing and that he took his traps with him, as well as other supplies and materials to make a skin boat. The implication is that Eppler hired Dalziel just for the flight in. Turner doesn't say how Eppler chose Rabbitkettle Lake. Others say that Dalziel recommended it, except it was Glacier Lake, and that he had a line there; the inference would be that Eppler and Mulholland were working for Dalziel. One possibility is that Dalziel had a line set up at Glacier Lake that he wanted worked.

There was a cabin and cache at Glacier Lake (Cormack mentions two cabins, but one with a caved-in roof). The plan was that after the trapping season ended, Eppler and Mulholland would build their boat and float down to Nahanni Butte with their winter's catch. As mentioned earlier, Faille assumed that they would either do this, or meet him at the mouth of the Flat, or walk from Glacier Lake to his cabin down Irvine Creek.

According to the police report, concerns about the men surfaced in mid- to late May. Turner agrees, putting it at the end of May. Jack Mulholland (brother of Bill) asked Dalziel to check on the men, and he reported that the cabin had been burned to the ground, with no trace of the men. Cormack reported that the cabin was intact.

The RCMP found out, probably from Dalziel flying into Fort Simpson to report on the trip he'd made at Jack Mulholland's request. The next day, Constable Graham had Dalziel fly him to the mouth of the South Nahanni, where he checked with Jack Mulholland and Poole Field. When Jack Mulholland requested a police search be made, Constable Graham flew to Glacier Lake with Dalziel and found nothing except a razed cabin. They couldn't land because they had floats on the plane and the lake was still frozen, so they couldn't poke around the rubble.

Everyone thought floating out on a skin boat was a stupid idea. Faille said it would be suicide. Eppler, Turner says, took canvas and paint along to make his boat.

In my view, Eppler either didn't know or had forgotten that the river is a nightmare of standing waves and whirlpools, from Virginia Falls to the mouth of the Flat. Patterson's map doesn't feature these. Also, in May, after the ice goes out there are still chunks of shore ice bobbing along, some of them quite large, not to mention trees that the flood has brought down into the river. These could easily take out a skin boat. It might have been for these reasons that Faille was expecting the two men to turn up at his cabin on Irvine Creek or to walk down the river to the mouth of the Flat.

Dalziel claims he had met Bill and George Cormack that winter in Fort Simpson. And after trapping all winter, the brothers returned to Nahanni Butte and found that Eppler and Mulholland hadn't yet arrived. They fired up the Curtis Robin and flew up the river and over to Glacier Lake. The RCMP don't have Cormack at Nahanni Butte at that time; they report Dalziel flying in by himself and that he found the cabin in ashes.

But according to Bill Cormack, he and Dalziel did land at Glacier Lake and the cabin was intact, as was the cache, but the furs were gone. Cormack says he walked down the creek from the lake toward the Nahanni River but found no packed snow or other evidence that the trappers had been snowshoeing in that direction. Presumably this was when the "rubble" was searched. According to Turner, "no bodies were found inside, the traps were gone and there was no rifle or axe in the burned cabin."

The RCMP has Cormack going in on June 6- 9, which fits with Cormack's description of when he went in. The report says, "Dalziel and his partner, Bill Cormack, made a further air search of the whole area between June 6 and 9, but failed to locate any trace of the pair. They did decide, however, that neither Eppler nor Mulholland perished in the cabin fire."

So, did Cormack go in twice? And why does he emphatically say in his interview that the cabin was there and in his report to police that it wasn't?

Shortly after, the RCMP interviewed Faille and Kraus, learning that Dalziel had told them, in March, that Eppler and Mulholland "would be coming out overland from Glacier Lake through the pass to Irvine Creek and overland again to the Flat River." Turner comes in on this, figuring that Eppler, being fearless, might have walked down the river on the ice, which was unsafe. Or wolves might have gotten them.

To add one last note: police reports from November 1964 state that Eppler and Mulholland were actually at Bennett Creek during that winter and in spring, on their way out, and they may have been caught in a landslide. A slightly earlier report, filed in October 1964, states that the two were on the Flat River at the time of their disappearance. But this is almost 30 years after the fact, and the police may have wanted to close the file.

A year after Eppler and Mulholland went missing, according to Dalziel, he and Nazar Zenchuk found remains of a canvas-covered camp above the falls. They believed the canvas belonged to Eppler and Mulholland.

But Zenchuk says he found the campsite at the mouth of the Flat River, below the falls.

So, it all ends in total confusion. All we know is that Eppler and Mulholland disappeared.

But we don't even know that for sure. In January 1938, Andy Wittington told Dick North he had seen Eppler in Vancouver, and "with that one eye and pug nose of his, I never could be mistaken."

North's theory is that Eppler was on his way to Australia.

CHAPTER 5

TRACES OF TRAPPERS

Leaving extra food and gear in the cabin on the Flat Lakes, John, Shea and I loaded our packs and walked around the bottom of the lake to the conservation officer's cabin, where John found a shed full of wood, and a chopping block near the door with an axe parked in the block. Shea found a second shed, with quad tracks leading out of it and toward the lake.

I examined the tiny cabin, grossly overprotected from what we assumed to be a possible grizzly bear attack. There were sheets of plywood, each of which had at least a hundred large nail spikes sticking outward, covering the door and window, and the door also had a crude painting of a grizzly's head.

"This guy's really paranoid," said John. "I can see he'd imagine being ambushed."

John and Shea examining the conservation officer's cabin.

"There's a freezer back here," Shea said from behind the woodshed. "There's nothing in it."

"If he sees us, he'll pull out his gun," I said. "Let's go."

I walked through a field of poppies that extended beyond the shack and onto the road to a rock bluff and found, behind it, our road to Zenchuk Creek. I started up the hill, but John and Shea were far too interested in the living conditions of the conservation officer to follow me, so I sat on my pack and waited until, finally, feeling guilty, John started up the trail toward me, and Shea, not comfortable with being alone yet, followed John.

After four hours of uphill hiking featuring vistas of the Flat Lakes, we came to a picnic table, a relic from the days when the miners were still working in the town and using the area for recreation. It sat in a turn-around area that overlooked the lake. From the table, we picked a distant landmark part way up Zenchuk Creek, set our compass and started bushwhacking uphill, through tall, thick willow and scratchy dwarf birch.

John & Shea are a bit exhausted after uphill hiking to Zenchuk Creek.

Unlike Dalziel when he did his momentous hike to Fort Norman on the Mackenzie River, we couldn't find any animal trails to follow. The day was hot and the bugs buzzed, looking for blood. They'd never seen such soft-skinned donors before!

It took a tough three hours to get into the alpine, where wildflowers were under our feet and a refreshing breeze kept the bugs at bay. Storm clouds formed quickly. Sometimes they drenched us with solid sheets of water, and other times, they merely threatened and teased us as they rolled past.

Farther up the valley we found a rocky outcropping and, at its base, a tin of safflower oil rusting in the sun. Although this type of oil has been found in Egyptian tombs, we knew that our find, in a modern-day container, was probably left here in the 1950s or maybe even later. It was full, and the seal on its lid had never been broken.

CHAPTER 5: TRACES OF TRAPPERS

We continued past a waterfall with foaming water crashing down three giant steps. Then, near the head of the valley, we came to a clearing that had an old rusting stove, a few flat spots for tents, a Swede saw hanging from a nail in a tree, a pressure cooker, a plate and some wire.

Saw and pan found at an old campsite on the upper end of Zenchuk Creek.

John and Shea rooted around, scattering the rusted tin cans and partly broken bottles that bordered the camp, and I hauled wood from the edge of the forest for a campfire. Shea held up a stovepipe, and John de-crimped it to protect the fire from any rain that might fall. As we ate supper, we speculated on who might have lived here before. I favoured Zenchuk.

The following morning, we walked toward what looked like a rock wall on the pass leading to the Rabbitkettle River. Along the way we came to a creek with milky water, but it didn't feel much warmer than the water in the main creek, so we assumed it was not runoff from the hot spring rumoured to be in the area. At the pass we trekked around the wall and stared at the impenetrable blanket of spruce trees below. We knew that bushwhacking through that in an attempt to reach the Nahanni River and the Rabbitkettle Hot Springs would take days and days. I wondered how Dalziel had done it when he entered the valley from Hole-in-the-Wall Lake.

Inspired, we left Zenchuk Creek, our plans for the following summer roughed out. We'd go farther north next time, along the Little Nahanni River, and then head for some dots that appeared on the map just west of the South Nahanni. Once back in Tungsten, Gerald told us that the dots to the north were at Howard's Pass and the dots to the east indicated the Union Carbide Exploration site.

CHAPTER 6

HISTORY OF HOWARD'S PASS

Mining in the Nahanni area, the territory of the expanded park itself and the entire drainage area of the South Nahanni River, starts with placer gold mining by the First Nations on what came to be called the Bennet, Borden, Gold and McLeod Creeks just off the Flat River. This history is too colourful, as R M Patterson seemed to think, to be entirely believable. As he put it, "it rivals anything that even Jack London's fertile imagination could bring forth." But the instigating involvement of the First Nations is believable. They often came out to Nahanni Butte and Fort Simpson with placer gold as well as fur.

Eventually the spot was found, evidently, and mined with the sluice boxes left there by the First Nations. Patterson says the lucky fortune hunters filled "a tooth-ache remedy bottle of gold." But over the next few years that was magnified a thousand times and a few wild "gold rushes" into the area took place.

Howard's Pass was one of many routes of the Indigenous peoples through the divide from Yukon into the upper Flat. Since they were known to trade gold as well as fur, they certainly would have checked Steel Creek on their way to the Liard and Mackenzie, and many white prospectors, most of them mainly trappers, would have followed along behind them, right to the present time.

But there is much more than gold in the mountains along the divide. First came tungsten, right at the headwaters of the Flat, and then further north at Macmillan Pass, the route of the Canol pipeline.

Then came lead-zinc, at Howard's Pass, which after a few years of exploration was claimed to be the richest lead-zinc deposit in the world.

Here, I must make a comment on the history of mining operations in the South Nahanni River drainage. It seems to me that the modern ones are as legendary as the ones that Patterson described. There are claims being made about, and tremendous amounts of human energy expended over, what? Little or nothing, so the history tells us. The wealth to be taken from the mountains of the territorial divide, from the headwaters of the Flat through Howard's Pass to Macmillan Pass, is mythical in the sense that very little has ever come of it. The mine at Tungsten did operate for a while, but never amounted to much considering the deposits there, and operations to the north never got beyond exploration despite the apparent surges of activity. This includes companies buying the deposits from one another, and companies in court with the local governments, First Nations people and the park over environmental problems only to be replaced by other companies. It also includes large areas explored without any idea of how they could be exploited, and huge deposits announced followed by the discovery that they are not huge enough to warrant the expense of exploiting them.

The imagination of a Jack London indeed!

But maybe that's the mining business. I'll do my best, as Patterson tried to do his best concerning the Flat River rush of January, 1934, to deal with mining in the divide, focussing on Howard's pass. But I'm afraid I'm describing, in Patterson's words a series of "episodes of romantic buffoonery."

Access road to Howard's Pass. It runs above the Flat Lakes.

In 1968, Placer Dome Development Ltd. had a team of prospectors testing stream sediments in the Howard's Pass area, northwest of the Flat Lakes. Placer Dome found large deposits of zinc-lead. During the 1970s, they built an access road to Howard's Pass that wound above the west shore of the Flat Lakes and continued due north, skirting the Little Nahanni River as far as Steel Creek, where the road then ran northwest

CHAPTER 6: HISTORY OF HOWARD'S PASS   **65**

to Howard's Pass. Four years after Placer found the zinc-lead deposit, the company staked claims and conducted extensive sample drilling until late 1981.

They announced a mine would open at the site if both underground and open-pit mines together would produce 20,000 tons of minerals per day for a period of 20 years. But exploration and planning stopped because the cost of mining in that location was exorbitant, due to lack of power and road access. Placer Dome packed up their gear and left a mess.

This is where we came in, during the summer of 1995. As usual, John found the mess far more interesting than the hike. Once home, I wrote newspaper articles that caught the attention of officials and environmentalists, and eventually the site was cleaned up, including the mining engineer's cabin that John had fixed up. His heart is still broken.

In June 2000, Placer sold its claims to Copper Ridge Explorations and Cygnus Mines. The new owners then signed an agreement with Billiton Metals to evaluate and develop the property. In October, they drilled eight holes and found an even higher concentration of zinc and lead than had been found in the 1970s. But in December, Copper Ridge claimed it couldn't pay Placer Dome for the rights on the claim. During the next four years, while the companies figured out what should be done, the site lay dormant.

Placer Dome and Cygnus agreed to try again. In April 2005, Pacifica Resources, a company formed in 2004 after the reorganization of Expatriate Resources, which had interests in the Howard's Pass/Macmillan Pass projects, joined the team with an understanding that Pacifica and Expatriate could, if they desired, purchase 100 percent of the property within seven years. The group drilled a total of 1,695 samples and found numerous zones over a distance of 30 kilometers that were suitable for mining. The following year, that distance was expanded to 37 kilometers, and the new information showed a higher mineralization content than first thought when the area was explored between 1969 and 1981.

Based on the new studies, Pacifica stated that there were 55 billion pounds of zinc and 20 billion pounds of lead at Howard's Pass, making this the richest zinc-lead site in the world. Besides the fifteen deposits of zinc and lead found, the area also had copper, silver, tungsten, gold, vanadium, barite and gemstones waiting to be plucked out of the ground.

In May 2007, Pacifica Resources became Selwyn Resources. At this point, the company had spent about $100 million on exploration in the area. Some of that money was used in restoring the area to its natural state. In 2008 the company received Yukon's prestigious Leckie Award for extensive reclamation work at Howard's Pass and for providing environmental education to community members in Ross River. The award is presented once a year to companies that have exhibited outstanding reclamation and restoration efforts and/or for exceptional social responsibility. In this case, Selwyn won in both areas. I like to think that our articles and photos helped spark this reclamation.

In 2010, Selwyn signed an agreement with China's Yunnan Chihong Zinc and Germanium Co., Ltd. to invest an additional $100 million for more exploration work.

However, there were requirements to be met before the mining company could go ahead with production. First, a port for shipping had to be determined, with the possibilities being Haines and/or Skagway in Alaska, or Stewart in BC. For some reason, taking the ore out to Vancouver, as they had before the shut down of the Tungsten mill in 1986, was not considered. Anyway, at that time none of these ports had the capacity to accommodate the amount of ore the mine would ship to refineries in Russia. They also wanted to send low-grade tungsten by truck to Pennsylvania for processing.

Second, a source of energy, mainly to the new mill that would refine that ore, also needed to be found. The mine would be too far from the Spectra natural gas line in southeast Yukon. Besides, Spectra had ideas of possibly closing, which it did in 2012. The company also considered the gas line along the Mackenzie River, but this too would be expensive.

The only other options considered were using diesel or liquid natural gas, which would have to be transported into the site by truck, making it also very expensive.

Third, a mode of delivery to the port also had to be considered. The road built in the 1970s, that started at the Robert Campbell Highway and ran over the Nahanni Range Road, then north to the pass, would require upgrading. The all-weather road, to be used all year, would need to be upgraded to accommodate the added heavy-vehicle traffic. The estimated cost for building the road and putting a mine into production was believed to be about $1.8 billion.

However, nothing could happen without consultation and approval from the local First Nations. Since Nahanni National Park had been formed and at this point (see Chapter 16) there were plans to expand its borders, the road would pass through a small section of the park before it reached Howard's Pass. Both Parks and the Kaska Dene Nation were troubled about the air and water pollution that a mill of this size would create. But their biggest concerns involved the potentially dangerous effects of lead, transported through the water systems, on human and animal life.

The Kaska-Dene had already been through pollution problems with the mine at Tungsten; the massive settling pond was seeping pollutants into the Flat River. Back in 2000, the mine at Tungsten reopened after 15 years of being dormant. This reopening occurred without inspection of the site but the company posted a $900,000 security bond for the existing water licence. When a fuel spill occurred in January, 2001, this bond was worth one-tenth of the amount required to clean it up. In 2003 the company re-negotiated a five-year water contract that required Cantung to post a total of $9 millions in securities. None of this money was ever provided because they couldn't agree on whether the water licence was in effect when the mine was not operating.

The Kaska-Dene took Selwyn Chihong to court and, in August 2011, Judge Ron Veale dismissed the case, claiming the company would monitor their own activities. Under the government of the Stephen Harper

Conservatives, that was the song of the day—that companies would be responsible and police themselves.

In an appeal, the Kaska Dene in conjunction with Park officials returned to court, fighting over the safety of the environment from spills and adverse impacts on wildlife, and more specifically, the threat that traffic would present to already endangered herds of caribou in the area. There was also the problem of invasive plants being introduced to the park, plus damage to cultural and archaeological sites by exploring humans. Both Mactung and Tungsten sat dormant while laborious negotiations continued.

Then in 2013, Selwyn Resources signed an agreement with Chihong Canada to share a purchase agreement for Selwin's remaining 50 percent joint-venture interest in all the projects along the divide between Mac Pass and Tungsten. Selwin would get $50 million. This agreement included the approval of the Environmental Assessment Board and the obtaining of a water-use license. If Chihong Canada, a subsidiary of the Yunnan Chihong Zinc & Germanium Co., Ltd. became the sole owner of the project, this would result in it being the second Chinese company to have control of a large Yukon mine. This is interesting because one of the reasons for closing the Tungsten mine in 1986 was that the Chinese were subsidizing their own production and putting Canada out of the game.

The companies proposed production at Howard's Pass would be about 3,500 tonnes per day from the underground mine and 25,000 tonnes per day from the open-pit mine. Chihong went ahead and upgraded the road in 2014 so it could take traffic from about 100 loaded trucks coming and going each way, every day. But the price of tungsten was dropping on the international market, which evidently made the lead-zinc project at Howard's Pass less feasible. The upgraded and extended road may have been more of a selling feature than a move towards opening the mines.

Due to environmental issues and the costs involved in getting the ore out to the freighters in Vancouver, the mine remained in the hands of North American Tungsten who then put the company up for sale. The selling price was anywhere between $2.5/$4.5 million (depending on sources) and the North American Tungsten Corporation eventually became the property of the federal and territorial governments. Tungsten Corp. filed for bankruptcy, thus releasing itself from the financial responsibility for cleaning up the two sites. This then became an expensive deal; as of 2019 the federal government has spent about $32.4 million, while the territorial government has contributed about $208,000, maintaining the sites to the satisfaction of the Mackenzie Valley Land and Water Board. So far, even though prices are rising for tungsten, there has been no production from either mine-site, and the for-sale sign is still swinging in the winds.

As a result of numerous mines being abandoned in the territories, the Northern Abandoned Mine Reclamation Program was formed in conjunction with the Indigenous, and northern communities in an attempt to improve the statutes like the NWT Water's Act, the Mackenzie Valley Resource Management Act and the Territorial Lands Act. The main purpose of the program was to give the territorial governments and their people more power to protect land and water from pollution and to obtain financial security for reclamation. In the end, laws protecting the land were strengthened but little legal leverage was obtained for enforcing reclamation.

After years of negotiations and development, the Department of Indian Affairs and Northern Development (DIAND) took over the "drafting of terms and conditions of regulatory instruments," which finally resulted in stronger laws being passed to prevent land use abuses in all land-use contracts.

But there were still old sites that had no protection so DIAND now manages the remediation of eight abandoned mines in Yukon and Northwest Territories. In 2019 it was allocated a $2.2 billion budget to be used over 15 years starting in 2020-21. In the NWT, Cantung Mine Project, which includes both Tungsten and Macmillan Pass sites, are part of the projected cleanup. This seems like a pittance as compared to the $18 billion received from the mining of metal and minerals in the territories since 1977.

CHAPTER 7

ELSEBETH AT HOWARD'S PASS 1995

As it turned out, our friend Shea went tree-planting for the summer, but lucky for John and me, our Danish friend, Elsebeth Vingborg, who had hiked numerous times with us in Kluane, wanted a summer of adventure, so we planned on going to Howard's Pass in the Tungsten/Nahanni area.

On our way, we found no changes along the Nahanni Range Road. The washout was just as boisterous, but this time we'd stuck a canoe on the roof of our truck alongside the bicycles. John crossed with a heavy pack holding him down and a rope attached to the canoe. Then we loaded the boat and lined it across.

We used bikes to haul the canoe from the car to the washout.

The Pitts were home when we arrived. Gerald was busy hauling machines from the mine and medicine cabinets out of the miners' living quarters. Stan, the conservation officer, was on his quad, and our Flat Lakes Cabin was just as we'd left it, although the squirrels had resumed residence. We flattened pieces of tin and pounded them over holes under the eaves.

Our first day out, we cycled 28 kilometers to a trapper's cabin where Mac Creek flowed into the Little Nahanni. The road ran anywhere from a hundred to two hundred feet above the river and was in good condition, although many of the culverts from smaller creeks had washed out, leaving deep trenches across the road.

The cabin was unlocked but full of plywood boxes, used for holding traps. No squirrel activity was evident; no shredded mattresses, no scat, no food on the floor. We dumped the traps outside and slept inside on bunks, with luxurious mattresses beneath us.

We enjoyed the comfort of a trapper's cabin.

The next morning, after storing the traps back inside the cabin and securing the door so it wouldn't blow open, we crossed our first bridge. It had been washed out on the far side and was buckled in the middle. After scrounging around, we found a solid plank, which we propped so that one end was on shore and the other against the bridge, to sort of bridge the gap so we could roll our bikes to the far side of the creek.

The next bridge, which was in good shape, carried us over Guthrie Creek, and the third bridge, at Fork Creek, was washed out at the south end, so we used the same technique as we had on our first bridge. Then, because it was so time-consuming and hard carrying gear and bikes over these bridges, we abandoned our bikes and started walking.

The road was bush-free, and the Little Nahanni River below snaked through the valley, its surface dotted with huge boulders. At one spot, we watched it enter a canyon and heard its threatening roar.

After securing a board to walk off the bridge, John carried the bike across.

March Creek had a good bridge where we had lunch, our pack contents spread over the bridge deck, stove and pot sitting level, our behinds comfortable on the 6-by-6 bridge edging. We found Steel Creek, the next waterway we had to cross, was more of a river, with a solid gravel bottom. It poured a lot of water through a number of braids into the Little Nahanni.

We had decided on Howard's Pass for the summer's destination, but we could see where a winter road crossed the river, just above Steel Creek, and entered the bush on the other side. How that opening beckoned! Being curious, we dropped packs and walked along the winter road down to the Little Nahanni, which was a good 40 feet across. Though it flowed smoothly over a flat stretch, it looked deep.

"We could float across in a rubber tube with a rope attached, sort of like a reaction ferry," I suggested.

"How about a pack raft?"

"They weigh a ton from what I understand, and I think they cost a fortune."

March Creek bridge where we enjoyed a lunch.

Machine shop at Howard's Pass.

CHAPTER 7: ELSEBETH AT HOWARD'S PASS 1995

We returned to the main road, which ran due west, up the south bank of Steel Creek, and then turned north and crossed over a solid, intact bridge.

It was raining as we approached Howard's Pass. John dully trudged along, not saying much, his arms crossed over his chest, his head down, probably creating a poem to keep his mind off the weather. Suddenly, as the road flattened out, he noticed the trail approaching a level area. He then saw a building in the distance and ran through a gully to get to it, his heavy pack bouncing on his hips. The building turned out to be a machine shop positioned on the edge of an airstrip.

I glanced at the junk in the machine shop and sat outside under the eaves on a backless chair that was far more comfortable than anything I'd felt since we left the Flat Lakes. John pulled out some corrugated steel from the shop and built a campfire, using the sheets to protect the fire from wind and rain. He found a grill to place our pots on and then he located two more chairs. But the rain increased, so we hustled inside, where we found one wall lined with steel bed frames. We dropped our packs on the first one and speculated that hunters must have stayed in the building to protect themselves from the wind. But for me, the building was too big and cold to be inviting.

The sun came out, the shop warmed and we unpacked our wet gear and spread it out on the beds to dry. John kept scrounging around, looking for pieces of leftover junk to make his camping life more civilized.

With lunch and coffee break over, I left John and Elsebeth napping and walked further along the valley, past neat piles of timbers, to an abandoned mining exploration site. As I explored, I saw a tunnel dug into a bluff on the other side of a raging creek. On my side of the creek, I noticed another machine shed with some tools, some of them useful, like an axe and a shovel, which I grabbed. A short distance farther, I spotted a shack with the door torn off but the windows, walls and roof still intact. Inside on the floor was paper, plastic, insulation and animal scat six inches deep. I ran back to the hangar and excitedly told John we had a cabin.

We donned our packs, and John followed me to our new home. It took him just a moment to see the potential. He grabbed the shovel I'd found and then scooped out the scat and took the chemical barrels to a second shed that also had an open door. Elsebeth and I picked up the papers and plastic core-sample bags, hung some of our things on nails and put the "No Smoking" signs in the windows. We helped John replace the ripped insulation and nail the plastic vapour barrier back to the studs, and then John rebuilt the door.

John repairing the Potato Hill cabin.

On the gravel parking area in front of the cabin, John built a firepit and framed it with two sawhorses, onto which he leaned a sheet of plywood to protect the fire from the wind—which seemed, in that spot, to howl incessantly.

Back at the building near the airstrip we collected the chairs, a broom, a pail for water, a coffee pot, a fry pan and nails. On our return to the cabin, we felt and looked like Ma and Pa Kettle moving from the Ozarks. However, by supper the cabin was clean and we were able to put our sleeping bags on the floor. The radio code name, Potato Hill, became our new cabin's name. It was also written in one of the books the previous tenants had neglected to shred, and above the window was the radio licence with Yukon Government permit # 981.

Early next morning, John started pounding sheets of roofing material along the outside wall of the cabin, much to the disgust of the ground squirrel perched underneath. There was enough aluminum sheeting and three-quarter-inch plywood to cover the entire shack three feet up from the ground, which would prevent the animals from chewing the wood and re-entering the building after we left. We washed clothes and hung them on the radio towers lying at the side of the cabin.

A three-inch propane furnace chimney outlet was in the wall, so John hunted around and found an old airtight stove and pipes, which had to be adapted in size from six inches at the stove to three inches at the wall. He clamped the pipes together using hose clamps found in the boiler shed. Being paranoid about fire, he lined the ceiling with fiberglass insulation and finished the chimney with a second three-inch pipe rising above the roof.

The stove produced just enough heat in the cabin to carry the chill and dampness away and made sleeping more comfortable than in the tent. Once again, we were in a cabin, just as John had hoped we'd be throughout most of our hikes. Early the following morning, while I was still nestled tight in my sleeping bag, John made coffee. After I got up, we sat sipping our brew in the morning sun at the side of the cabin and watched two wolves—close to three feet at the shoulder, a silver tip and a blonde—come over the hill towards us. They were checking out marmot mounds and gopher holes, looking like two teenagers out for a romantic stroll. Then suddenly they stopped, looked at the cabin, sniffed at the air and made a quick detour toward the northern hills.

John stands proudly in his renovated cabin.

After breakfast, we went exploring. We had seen a tower on the mountain to the north of the pass, so we climbed in that direction. At the top, we found a radio or microwave tower, a wooden box full of twelve-volt batteries, and an aluminum stepladder. Elsebeth climbed the ladder and posed for a photo.

To the north we could see Mount Wilson at the headwaters of the South Nahanni River, and beyond that, we knew was the Canol Pipeline, started during the Second-World War to facilitate the movement of high-grade oil from Norman Wells to Whitehorse. But before the pipeline could be built, a road was needed. The government, in its haste to get the job done, started one end of the road at Norman Wells and the other in Whitehorse. The two ends met at Macmillan Pass, in the direction we were looking.

Elsebeth sitting on a ladder to get a better view of Mount Wilson at least 100 kilometers farther north.

After lunch, we checked out more of the mining exploration remains on and around the pass. The mess was extreme. We found tons of jelled material, used to fill holes in rock made from the diamond drilling. The material was bursting from its burlap containers onto the ground. In a small shed was a stonecutter with its electric motor removed, and glass containers of high-molarity acids; the strong acids were welding the lids of the containers to the necks of the bottles. Someone had burnt a row of bunkhouses and lined up about two dozen folding bedframes on their sides. There were rows upon rows of core sample containers and hundreds of 45-gallon fuel containers, mostly empty.

Gel used to fill holes made by drilling core samples.

Oil barrels, some full and others empty.

A sewage lagoon and the ruins of a washhouse were close to the creek, and there was an ore-car rusting on the road. We crossed the creek and entered the tunnel, pulling aside the ragged blue plastic tarp fluttering in the wind. At the partly boarded-up entrance we found some hardhats and rubber outfits hanging from pegs. The ground was saturated with oil, and a stream of water flowed from beneath the boards into the main creek.

The tunnel entrance open and accessible.

While John did more construction to our cabin, Elsebeth and I went exploring south of the pass and far above the road we had followed on our way in. We also hiked north, where our road went for a short distance past the exploration site and then dwindled into the bush.

Two days later, we turned back south, overland across alpine meadows, towards Summit Lake. One meadow we walked through had a herd of grazing caribou, and two curious youngsters came close enough for us to touch. We clicked the cameras instead. Then, with the lake visible in the distance, we pondered the bushwhack we would have to do to get there. But we turned east instead and crossed a small pass down to the road again.

After two rest days at the Flat Lakes cabin, we headed out to Watson Lake for burgers, beer and fries—salt and fat.

CHAPTER 8

HISTORY OF UNION CARBIDE

Our contours of the area around the Little Nahanni River showed buildings to the east, past Dozer Lake and Lened Creek (marked as hot springs) and into the hills halfway between the Little Nahanni and the South Nahanni rivers. Gerald had identified it as a Union Carbide exploration site.

I associated Union Carbide, a subsidiary of Dow Chemical Co. since 2001, with the deadly gas-leak disaster in Bhopol, India, in 1984, where over half a million people were exposed to the lethal methyl iso-cyanate gas. It killed 4,000 people instantly and 15,000 over the next few years, from lingering effects. I had seen some of the results of this disaster when I visited India and knew that Dow was still in court disputing the court order to pay settlements of $25 to each of the victims. And now, the same company was working in one of the most pristine and remote parts of Canada, about which I was possessive. I wanted to see their site.

During our winter research, through the pamphlet files at the Vancouver library, we found that prospectors working for Canex Aerial Exploration Ltd. first explored the Lened Creek area in 1960. The following year, a syndicate was formed with Centennial Mines and Canadian Exploration Ltd. They did mapping, surface sampling and some drilling, but the price of tungsten and copper fell, so the claims lapsed.

John Harris at the Lened Creek Hot Springs.

In 1967 the area was re-staked by Hugo Brodell and then transferred to Atlas Explorations the following year. The claim reverted to Brodell and then, in 1973, was taken over by Canex Placer, but again returned to Brodell within the year. Union Carbide purchased claims from Brodell in 1977 and staked 227 more claims. It did mapping, soil sampling and surveying from 1977 to 1979 and had an environmental assessment done in 1980 by Envirocon Ltd. to look at the distribution of Dall sheep, caribou and moose populations in the Selwyn Mountains and what impact a mine would have on these animals.

By the end of 1982, just under 170 holes had been drilled. The site we were hoping to reach was probably where the core samples would be located. But no development occurred. At this time, a 500-ton-a-day mill, employing 120 people, was projected. Then in 1996, Ron Berdahl, who had worked for Union Carbide during the early explorations at Lened Creek, re-staked the claim. Because of the limestone lenses in the Lened area, similar to those at Tungsten, the company expected to find some garnet.

Finally, in 2006 Playfair Mining took 100 percent possession of the Lened property, and in 2016, it deemed the site a historic resource. In other words, Playfair owns the rights to the site's minerals, but has left it dormant.

CHAPTER 9

UNION CARBIDE HIKE 1996

Going to the Union Carbide site required fording the Little Nahanni, a river that even the famous Canadian paddler Bill Mason had said was tough. We believed him. We had listened to the river the year before and seen parts of it.

We thought we could be in trouble when we reached the washout on the Nahanni Range road, where what we saw indicated that what we'd heard was true—the winter's snowfall had been larger than usual, making the runoff heavier. June and July had been rainy, too.

But we were prepared again with canoe and rope, and again Elsebeth had come from Denmark to join us. With John on shore, holding the rope attached to one end of the canoe, Elsebeth and I paddled, using strong strokes, to get to the far side. Once there, Elsebeth grabbed the second attached rope and jumped ashore. After unloading our packs, we let John haul the canoe back across. He loaded the remaining gear, including our bikes, and climbed in. Placing his paddle carefully so the canoe wouldn't be washed downstream, he signalled for Elsebeth and me to pull the second rope. It worked like a Swiss watch.

We then cycled over the pass and up to the Flat Lakes, a familiar trip now. The road on the pass had a few more sinkholes, but any boulders that might have fallen onto the road were pushed to the side, a sign of regular comings from and goings to Tungsten.

At the end of two days hard travelling, we found ourselves huddling in the little trapper's cabin, listening to the rain drumming on the tin roof. We hoped and hoped that it would stop. But it didn't. The rain accompanied us all the way as we cycled and pushed our loaded bikes to the Little Nahanni River at the confluence of Steel Creek. The three bridges we'd crossed the year before had survived. Even our planks were in the bush where we'd left them.

Once at the Little Nahanni, we found we couldn't go straight across but there was a gravel bar in the center of the river.

To get to the bar, we had to follow a submerged spit that had been formed in a back eddy and just a few feet upstream from the gravel bar. Once at the gravel bar we had about 100 feet of river to cross, with 80 feet being in swift current.

Our plan was that John would cross from the bar to the far side first. If he couldn't make it, neither would Elsebeth or I. Because I was the shortest and lightest, I was the weakest of the group, especially when it came to crossing.

At the gravel bar, John attached a rope to his pack and Elsebeth held the other end while I stood watching. John entered the water with his loaded pack, unbuckled in case he got swept away. He put his pole at an angle of about 40 degrees to his body and sidestepped slowly into the current.

The ice water lapped at his stomach and hips, making him gasp. He needed his heavy pack to keep his feet on the bottom, even though the weight in the unbuckled pack was throwing him off-balance. The rope sagged into the water and pulled him downstream. He shouted for Elsebeth to let go of the rope. It was not, as it turned out, long enough to reach the other shore anyway. I stood at the edge of the water, timing John's crossing. It took three minutes and 15 seconds of struggle to reach the calmer water near the far shore.

John Harris crossing the Little Nahanni River.

Relieved, I watched as John emptied his pack onto the beach, hauled in the rope and dropped some boulders into the pack for weight. The plan was that I would cross behind him in the little eddy formed from his body blocking the rushing water. He reached the gravel bar and danced around, trying to get feeling back into his toes. We then transferred some of the weight out of my pack into his and entered the cold water. I was terrified. I didn't have a stick. One step out of place or one slippery rock and we'd be swept away. While consciously staying in the eddy, I balanced myself by holding John's hip belt. At one point, I moved too quickly and the current pushed me off-balance. My movement threw him off-balance too, but he managed to keep us from going over. We stood until we collected our calm and then, on John's command, we continued, yelling at each other over the roar of the water. About ten feet from shore, John got a cramp in his calf. He stopped and stretched his leg to alleviate the cramp and then yelled for me to take another step.

Once across, we flopped onto the ground with our backs to the river. Kicking our wet shoes off, we turned our attention to Elsebeth as she entered the water and worked her way, step by tiny step, just as we had done, moving across the current, the water slapping her stomach. I watched, barely breathing in fear that my gush of air would push her over. She hit shore and dropped, pack still on her back, hands shaking. John handed her a chocolate bar.

I stared back at the water. "What if it rises before we return?"

We went about a kilometer from the Little Nahanni River along the winter road, which turned out to be clear of underbrush. We found a comfortable camp spot and, after a quick dinner, tucked in for a cozy night's sleep, with raindrops tapping on the tent.

The next morning, full of porridge and expectations for the new country ahead, we followed the road up-valley toward Dozer Lake. It was still raining and there was some underbrush spreading onto the road, making us even wetter. By lunchtime, we were soaked and far less enthusiastic than we had been in the morning. We stopped on a flat gravel beach on a no-name creek that flowed into Dozer and put up the tarp. John built a fire so we could dry some of our things and have a hot lunch.

Four hours later, after we'd finished drying out, it was too late to continue, so we pitched tents and slept restlessly. The following morning, we got up late, and while eating breakfast, we looked in silence at the creek through the thick blanket of rain.

Bored with the immobility, we stoked the fire and dried our sleeping bags, our tents and anything else that was still damp. This took till noon. Once across what we took to calling Dozer Creek, we walked—or rather, trudged—for about six hours, climbing up a hill and over snot moss (our name for Cladina moss, which gets slippery when wet) to get above tree line. Finally, wet, cold and miserable, we silently dropped into the Lened Creek valley and made camp. Supper and bed came without much conversation.

Viv standing on Drill Creek Pass and pointing to Dozer Lake in the distance.

The following morning, forty-eight hours after the rain had started, it finally stopped. We took another four hours drying everything. Now in better spirits, we started up Lened Creek.

Before we'd gone far, we noticed green strips of vegetation as bright as neon flowing down the mountain. We found the vegetation hid a trickle of water. I dipped my fingers into the water and instantly pulled them out. We had found the Lened Creek hot spring, one we knew nothing about. There were a few pieces of lumber and plywood around, indicating that maybe prospectors had tried to pool the water at one time, but nothing permanent remained. I dropped my pack and pulled out the cooking pot so we could splash in hot wash water, so refreshing after the cold rain. Once warmed and our humour restored, we continued on to Union Carbide.

For most of the day, it rained intermittently, but we could see the clouds breaking. Late in the afternoon, we reached Union Carbide, with four collapsing core-sample racks and a few soggy sheets of plywood scattered around the alpine. I was ecstatic. Four intriguing passes leading from the site seemed to beckon me. I hardly noticed that the expected cabins and exploration junk was missing. But my companions noticed, pointing out three brown squares on the alpine where the cabins had been burned.

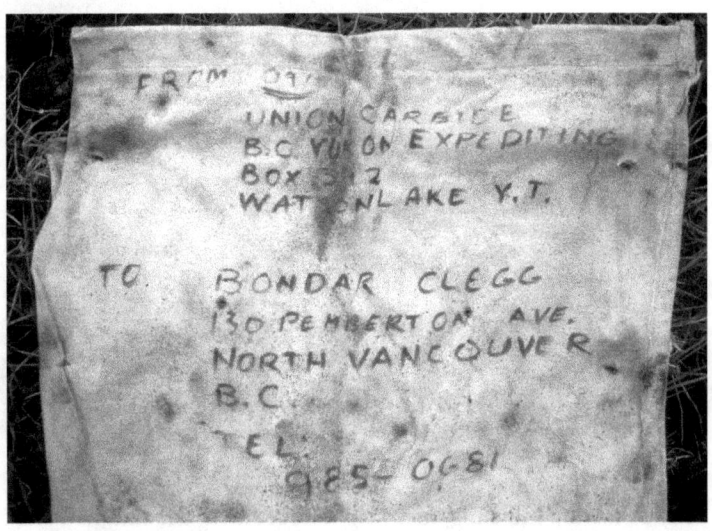

Core Sample bag found at Union Carbide. Telephone area code indicates the bag was used before 1996.

I dropped my pack and started walking this way and that, not sure which pass to check out first. We were in soft, rolling alpine, dotted with red flowers, and we had at least ten days in which to explore. I could hear John calling but I didn't care. I ran like a child.

When I finally returned to John and Elsebeth, waiting at the core sample racks, I saw sullen faces.

"There's another storm coming," John said, pointing at the black sky down valley.

"There're no cabins," added Elsebeth. "We're leaving."

"Leaving? No way!"

I looked around desperately.

"There's plywood. We can make a shelter."

But John and Elsebeth weren't listening. They were putting on their packs.

"There's no water."

"The creek is only five minutes away, and it's overflowing," I replied, pointing down the hill. "I'll haul all the water you need."

"There's no wood."

"There are old mine posts." I was frantic. I ran and picked up a post. "We can use them."

"We need to get under cover before the storm hits."

I followed my companions in disbelief. We walked to the first creek and pulled out the tarp for protection from the storm. It didn't do the trick, and the site wasn't as habitable as John had thought. We continued to the next creek, two kilometers away, where there were flat spots for the tarp and our tents. We hauled some wood to burn and silently changed into dry clothes.

John tried to get a fire going, but the alpine wood was wet and too concentrated, even though he had chopped it into coin-sized pieces. With difficulty we rehydrated some pea soup and silently spooned our cold supper into our mouths.

"Look," I said pointing at the map. "There's an easy ten-kilometer hike over the pass and back to this spot. Let's do that in the morning."

"We have no wood."

"There's a poplar grove over there," I said, pointing a little ways down the hill.

"There'll be good wood there."

"I'm sick of the rain."

"Well, I'm going to the pass tomorrow. I'd like you to join me."

I zipped up my sleeping bag and turned my back to John, indicating that any further discussion wasn't going to happen. The following morning, under cloudy skies, we gathered wood and piled it under the tarp before heading back up to the pass. Carrying only cameras and daypacks full of snacks and rain gear, I chattered and sang, appreciating every step on the alpine grass that flowed up the gentle hill. My plan was that if I could make today a good day, I could get John and Elsebeth to go to a second pass tomorrow. I looked at the sky, dotted here and there with blue. The mountain gods were cooperating!

Chestnut Grizzly.

Then, about half a kilometer above the core-sampling racks, I looked up and saw a chestnut bear, his body turned sideways, his fur glistening, as he grazed on the flowers in the middle of the pass. I stopped.

"It's a bear," I whispered. "A beauty. Chestnut. Look at him."

But John and Elsebeth had already turned back.

"Oh! Come on! He's beautiful!"

Then I felt drops of rain. I walked, taking tiny steps, hoping to delay the rainstorm. Elsebeth was already packed and ready to leave when I arrived at the camp.

"No way," I cried, tears rolling down my cheeks. "We can't leave, after all it's taken to get here."

There was no argument. My companions were leaving. I couldn't stay by myself.

"Union Carbide cleaned up here better than they did in India ... The river will be high ... Next time I come back to Earth, I'm coming back as a man ... I think I see sun ... I hate quitters ... What makes men like Sir Richard Francis Burton? ..."

After a three-day walk, silent except for my muttering, we crossed the Little Nahanni again. The water was even higher, the crossing more dangerous, and I could no longer see the mountains surrounding Union Carbide. I stopped crying and started thinking about next year.

FURS AND MODELS

As we pedaled and pushed our bikes back to the Flat Lakes, a helicopter flew over us, circled back and hovered. We waved, and off it went. We spent a cozy, dry night in our cabin, had a leisurely breakfast and then loaded up and rode our bikes toward Tungsten. We planned to spend the day in or near the hot springs and then head back to the cabin for dinner.

Terry and Gerald were sitting at the picnic table when we got there and we joined them. A chopper landed and three young women, dressed in luxurious furs, emerged and three equally elegant women left the house and climbed into the plane.

"Models for a glossy New York catalogue," Terry said, nodding towards three anorexic girls, one black-skinned, one blond and one Asian, also dressed in long mink coats with fox collars.

"Each coat is worth about $60,000," Gerald said.

"They're being flown over to the glacier above Kuskula."

"And they're using your house as the dressing room?"

"Makeup and hair blowers are on every inch of the counter—and they expect me to feed them." Terry nodded at two gals standing near the cliff with earphones plugged in, drumming their hips to whatever music they had playing. They had no idea where they were, and they had no interest.

Gerald told us the rumour was that Nahanni Park's borders were to be expanded to the Flat River and that it would include the Cirque of the Unclimbables, just one or two valleys east of Tungsten. It would also include Hole-in-the-Wall Lake, located a few miles up a quad trail that ran on the north side of the Flat River. But the park wouldn't include the Flat Lakes.

"What about the Little Nahanni?" I asked. "It's getting popular with river rats."

"Not sure."

A consulting firm was doing a feasibility study, Gerald said, on the possibility of the abandoned mining town being converted into the Banff of the North. Apparently, everyone wanted to see a rich Japanese firm come in and convert the apartment buildings to hotel rooms, resurrect the recreational center, develop the hot springs and utilize other facilities to help make the project a success.

As we thought about the plan, making the town site a tourist draw seemed a reasonable proposition. Tungsten has 13 hot springs feeding the swimming pool. There are glacial-fed lakes within walking distance of the town site and hiking trails that were carved out by miners' wives, while their husbands worked, to surrounding peaks. These routes needed only a little trail clearing and a few directional signs to make them acceptable to the average hiker. In winter, the huge snowfalls could support a ski hill and cross-country skiing trips to some of the deserted cabins in the area, which could easily be upgraded. Some of the lakes are full of good-eating fish such as the arctic grayling, which in turn would attract many locals and even more tourists.

The old mineshaft could be used for historical tours, to illustrate what the inside of a mountain looks like, especially after man has been through it. There is also some gold in the area, which could attract tourist-prospectors.

Finally, the challenging Flat River was becoming increasingly popular among paddlers, and the Little Nahanni was being challenged by the more skilled and adventuresome. Canoeing the Flat or the Little Nahanni rivers from Tungsten to the South Nahanni and then out the Liard would be an attraction to many paddlers, and they wouldn't have to fly in. The possibilities were endless.

The cost, we thought, to convert the town into a resort wouldn't be that high. The road upgrade would need to take into account trailers and Winnebagos, but the airfield was in perfect shape and could be used immediately. The baseball diamond needed the grass cut and the swimming pool required some algae to be skimmed off the water before it was good to go, but those were minor requirements. The rec center would probably have to be totally rebuilt, but maybe not immediately.

When the park expanded in 2009, its size grew to 30,000 square kilometers, six times its original size, and it received National Park status in 2012. Tungsten wasn't included into the park, nor were the Flat Lakes, but all else east of the Yukon border including the Little Nahanni River was, as far north as Howard's Pass. The Moose Ponds area at the source of the South Nahanni River was also included, as were the Cirque of the Unclimbables and Glacier Lake. These features have been the main draw in this area for decades.

CHAPTER 10

HISTORY OF GLACIER LAKE

Since the First Nations people didn't build cabins and didn't venture far off the rivers, who built the cabins at Glacier Lake? Here are the possibilities—all white men.

First came the Klondikers in 1898. Patterson talks of how the Klondikers did an overland journey, coming from God knows where, lining their canoes up the Nahanni to the falls, portaging around the falls, and then what? Patterson describes the portage as a "trail that ran up a precipitous coulee: there were logs set across it for the skidding of a boat or a canoe, set there, perhaps, by the Klondikers—but those steps have vanished with the years and with the melting of twenty snows, for only Faille goes that way today."

The best route to the Klondike would have been up Rabbitkettle to the Flat Lakes and over the divide, or right up to the Moose Ponds, across from where the Canol Pipeline is now. Or, some of them got lost, or wintered over somewhere and never made it to the Glacier Lake. If some were explorers, the compelling Cathedral Mountain above Glacier Lake and at the entrance of the Cirque is visible from the Nahanni River.

Or Faille, of course. It's most likely—that explains the cabins. And then, for certain, Dalziel buzzing around and laying trap lines—but not, everyone said, building cabins. He would have had to do it in the year before he dropped Mulholland and Eppler at Glacier Lake. If he indeed dropped them there, and not at Rabbitkettle Lake.

Cathedral Mountain in 1939, before a huge slab fell off the side. With permission, the photo was copied at the Book and Record Depository at the University of Alberta.

What we know and what John and I found out through the most lucrative series of winter studies from 1993 to 1998 was published in numerous magazine and newspaper articles and in *Diary of a Lake, Tungsten John*, and in a fictional novel, *Above the Falls*. In our research, we heard about and got a look at Dalziel's notebooks. His granddaughter, Rebecca Bradford-Andrew, is working on a book using those notebooks.

First for us were the scientists, attracted to the Mackenzie Mountains because they were one of the last unstudied areas in North America. Glacier Lake was always the landing point, as it is at the center of the Mackenzie Mountains and big enough to get a loaded plane in and out. Some of these scientists, like Hugh Miller Raup, George W. Scotter, George Goodwin and Jim Soper, all published studies in prestigious journals.

With and after them came the climbers, such as Howard Fredrick Lambert, John Bailar, George Yntema, Dudley Bolyard, Bill Buckingham, Arnold Wexler, Donald Hubbard, and Sterling Hendricks. All were attempting to claim historical "first-routes" up the granite peaks of the Ragged Range.

Mountains south-west of Mt Sidney Dobson and across the Rabbitkettle River. Photo donated by H. Martyn.

With and after them, too, were the photographers, starting with Norm Thomas and followed by Peter Mather, Galen Rowell and Steve Brewis, who published images of never-before-seen mountains. These tales, reports and photographs have inspired others to see the river, to find a relic lost by some past adventurer, to climb a first route and possibly come close to adventure themselves.

Norm Thomas, the professional photographer who used a large format camera that remained undamaged while Thomas was on the raft, on the Nahanni River. Photo donated by H. Martyn.

There was even a novelist who in 1935 came to be the Governor General of Canada. Although he never set foot on the Nahanni, John Buchan, a.k.a. the first Baron of Tweedsmuir, became a popular writer in 1910. His most famous writings are *Thirty Nine Steps*, *Greenmantle* and *Mountain Meadow*. His last book, published in 1941, posthumously, was *Sick Heart*

River. It was reviewed favourably by Graham Greene. Buchan's river is believed to be the Nahanni. I read the book and it is obvious to me that if Buchan wasn't there, he knew someone who was, and that someone was Colonel Harry Michener Snyder.

COLONEL HARRY MICHENER SNYDER

According to Canadian historian Pierre Berton, Col. Harry Michener Snyder, was a wealthy big-game hunter who collected wildlife specimens for the American Museum of Natural History.

Berton, in *The Mysterious North*, claims Snyder was the first white man to visit Glacier Lake and in turn to see Cathedral Mountain and the Ragged Range. That visit was in 1934 and was strictly a reconnaissance mission.

Little is known about Harry Snyder, though if you took the time to read the documents and minutes of meetings connected to his numerous companies, you might get an inkling as to his personality. He was an Ohio-born oil magnate, Fellow of the Royal Geographical Society, Honorary Colonel of the Prince Edward Island Highlanders, holder of 27 rifle championships and, of course, a big-game hunter. He was also the author of a book about hunting that claims the sport will make men out of boys, and he was the leader of numerous hunting trips around the world.

He was featured in an article written by Harold Hilliard for *Pic Magazine* in June 1952, where Hilliard writes about Snyder's hunting escapades. The article claims that Snyder killed 736 big-game animals during his hunting years, including the oldest living mammal on the planet, an elephant that was said to be 175 years old and stood at 12 feet, 4 inches. Snyder kept the ivory tusks on display in his living room in Alberta and was photographed posing beside them. His biggest regret over hunting was he never got to shoot a grizzly bear with one shot. The closest he came was taking two shots to kill the most "dangerous target" on the planet.

Carrol Bates, Harry Snyder and Paul with trophy rams. Photo from Northern BC Archives, Prentiss Gray Collection, at UNBC.

Journeys in the Northwest Territories included shooting sheep in the lower Nahanni area and muskoxen east of Great Slave Lake. Because of his love of Canada's north and especially his love for big-game hunting, Snyder financed many scientific expeditions into the area, including into Glacier Lake. The hunting and scientific expeditions went together. Snyder had a long-standing deal with the National Museum of Canada (the predecessor to today's Canadian Museum of Nature and Canadian Museum of History) to provide specimens for display. Kraus claims that providing specimens made getting his hunting permits easier.

Snyder's attraction to the north started in 1926, when he and two American hunting friends arrived in my hometown of Prince George and then floated down the Crooked River just north of town and up the Parsnip, a river now flooded under the Peace Hydro Dam and Williston Lake. From the Parsnip, Snyder paddled into the Peace River and eventually landed at Hudson's Hope, where he met, as had been previously arranged, Jack Thomas, a hunting guide. But Thomas's camp crew had quit on him, so Snyder and his friends went up the Sikanni River and met up with the trapper, Jim Ross.

Harry Snyder cleaning his rifle. Photo from Northern BC Archives, Prentiss Gray Collection, at UNBC.

Snyder and Ross hit it off and, as the story goes, Snyder suggested that he and Ross go "dude wrangling" together. Ross accepted, thus beginning a successful 30-year relationship, whereby Ross eventually became the manager of Snyder's ranch in Sundre, Alberta. But they also agreed to go on a big hunt in the Peace region the following summer, in 1927. During this hunt, Snyder was treated to the gourmet cooking of Ted Boynton, who cooked for the 1927 hunt and all subsequent hunts through the 1930s.

CHAPTER 10: HISTORY OF GLACIER LAKE

In the stock-market crash of 1929, Snyder lost a lot of money, which in turn affected his health. His doctor suggested that his health would be restored if he took another northern hunting trip. Snyder contacted Ross and booked a hunt, as he did every summer for the next 20 years.

According to *Who's Who in Canada*, Snyder married Ida M. Shearer in 1911, and she probably accompanied him when he flew into Glacier Lake in 1934, the visit first mentioned by Pierre Berton. Snyder had a daughter, Dorothy, born in 1912, who was into filmmaking, and according to the *Yellowknife Blade*, she came to Yellowknife with her father in 1935. It doesn't seem that she was with him on the flight into Glacier Lake that year, but no one knows for sure. If she made a film, it has been lost to Canadian historians.

Snyder's business activities in the north are detailed in the book *North Again for Gold*, published in 1939, with Snyder's gold actually being uranium. He and Gilbert La Bine invested in the Eldorado uranium mine on Great Bear Lake, a subsidiary of the Eldorado Gold Mine founded by La Bine in his younger days as a prospector in the Ottawa Valley. La Bine became the president, and Snyder the treasurer. The refinery at Port Hope, Ont., was also financed by Snyder. But in 1942, the mine was expropriated, nationalized, and for security reasons, made into a crown corporation by the Canadian government. Shortly after, the refinery produced the uranium used in the top-secret Manhattan atomic bomb project in the United States.

The book *Eldorado* (1984) by Robert Bothwell explains the financing of the mine and refinery. That book also describes Lord Tweedsmuir's dealings with Snyder and makes fun of *North Again for Gold* as "one of the purest and most successful examples of company romanticism." Snyder's history with Eldorado is one of shady deals that resulted, ultimately, in disaster. In June 1939, he was kicked off the board.

Pierre Elliot Trudeau's father, Charles-Emile Trudeau, was a business affiliate and regular guest of Snyder's at Sundre. Trudeau, who owned a chain of Champlain gas stations, sat on the board of Champlain Oil, a company run by Snyder. The company and stations were later sold to Imperial Oil.

After meeting bush pilot Leigh Brintnell, Snyder invested in Mackenzie Air, an airline company out of Yellowknife for which Brintnell was general manager and number one flier. It is likely that Snyder heard about Glacier Lake from Brintnell, who'd been flying around the area since 1932.

It is not known who of Snyder's hunting team flew in on that 1934 reconnaissance trip, but mammalogist George Gilbert Goodwin, who was the assistant curator at the American Museum of Natural History in New York, did. Snyder's permits required the presence of a scientist. Goodwin filled the bill.

Colonel Mountain as seen from Glacier Lake. Photo donated by H. Martyn.

Although they stayed just a few hours, they took photos and named many of the prominent features. The Snyder Range was the name given to the surrounding group of peaks, and the strip of spruce-covered hills to the south of the lake was called Colonel Mountain, named after the man himself. Mount Ida, at the western end of the Snyder Range, was named

CHAPTER 10: HISTORY OF GLACIER LAKE

after his first wife. The creek flowing into and out of the lake and the glacier feeding the creek were all named after Brintnell. Red Mountain, at the top of Frost Creek, was named for the colour in the rock.

What is popularly known as Cathedral Mountain, located at the entrance to the Cirque, was renamed Harrison Smith by climber and surveyor Howard Fredrick Lambert in 1937. He was with Snyder then, and Harrison Smith was likely a friend of Snyder's. Lambert named the mountain after the president of Imperial Oil and International Petroleum Co. Ltd., and Harrison Smith is the name used on maps today. Brintnell Lake was renamed Glacier Lake, although the creek and glacier retained their original names. Mount Ida remained, but the Snyder Range became the Ragged. It might be a bit ironic that Ida, Snyder's first wife, remains snuggled up to Colonel Mountain, permanently perhaps, while Louise, his second wife, received no such honour, although she came to the lake with Snyder in 1952. Nor did his daughter Dorothy have her name attached to anything.

For Snyder's 1935 trip north, instead of going into Glacier Lake, he and Goodwin were east of Great Slave Lake, at Wood Buffalo National Park, at the west end of Lake Athabasca. In 1936, Snyder flew into Glacier Lake to take aerial photos, but weather prohibited any worthwhile photography. Snyder stayed three days and then left. Goodwin was in Asia that year.

During his 1937 excursion into the lake, Goodwin and Lambert were boated up from Fort Simpson with Ross as guide, Boynton as cook and George Roberts as river rat. Roberts piloted the boats up the Nahanni River to just below Virginia Falls. Lambert, who worked for the Geodetic Survey of Canada, mapped the area. He determined the height of the falls and established its exact geographical location.

Lambert had started surveying in 1917, but he was also a passionate climber, and president of the Alpine Club from 1924 to 1926. He is best known for climbing in the St Elias Range (now in Kluane National Park,) and was part of the first team to summit Mount Logan, the highest peak in Canada. Lambert published results of his studies of the Pacific Coast glaciers and explorations of Mount Logan, and he also published studies of the Rockies from Yellowhead Pass to Jarvis Pass in what is now Kakwa Provincial Park in B.C., about 200 kilometers east of Prince George. Besides recording geological information about the Nahanni River and Virginia Falls, he provided the exact geographical locations and altitudes of Mount Harrison Smith and Sidney Dobson, plus some of the peaks in the Cirque.

In 1937, it was Stan McMillan, of McMillan Air, who flew Snyder and Ida into Glacier Lake. Why Brintnell didn't fly them in is unknown. It is rumoured that Roberts climbed Cathedral Mountain with Lambert to set up a camera station as part of producing Lambert's topographical map of Glacier Lake. This is unlikely, but if it's true, it means that they were the first to climb in the cirque.

As soon as Snyder, Goodwin and Lambert arrived at the Glacier Lake campsite, they got to work. Goodwin trapped small animals, Snyder shot the large ones, and Lambert and his field assistant, Karl Stein of New York, took infrared photos and triangulation readings of the mountains. The data was to be used to produce the first contour map of the surrounding Mackenzie Mountains. Exact altitudes for some of the peaks in the Cirque were also recorded. During this trip, Snyder established that the Brintnell Glacier, one of the larger glaciers in the Ragged Range, was about 60 miles long and 30 wide, with 11 hanging and valley glaciers radiating off in all directions. His measurements of length and depth of the lake were corrected by a subsequent expedition. Snyder also overestimated the Brintnell Glacier, though it is hard to figure by how much, since it has shrunk considerably.

In his October 1937 publication in the *Canadian Geographical Journal*, Snyder boasts how he got into the canoe at Glacier Lake and chased a family of Canada geese to exhaustion for the "fun" of it, but to his credit, a few paragraphs after the goose chase, he stalked a moose grazing in Brintnell Creek and, rather than shooting it with his ever-present rifle, he filmed the animal eating.

Taken from Mount Ida and facing the Brintnell Glacier in the distance. Photo donated by H. Martyn.

Snyder and Ida left Glacier Lake after a week to meet Lord Tweedsmuir, Canada's Governor General at time, at the Eldorado Mines. This is when, I suspect, that Snyder, knowing Tweedsmuir was an author, whispered in his ear about the Nahanni area, the lost mine, supposed headhunting Indians, a temperate valley (Rabbitkettle Hot Springs), the cirque towers and the missing trappers.

Once they returned to their respective homes, Snyder and Goodwin published stories in *Natural History Magazine* about their adventures. Both articles, especially Snyder's, included photographs, and he described Cathedral Mountain as a "white granite peak that overshadows the upper end of the lake, its perpendicular walls towering over 4,000 feet."

According to Nazar Zenchuk, Snyder flew into Glacier Lake in 1938, this time with three Americans, and Jim Ross as guide and Boynton as cook. At that time, not much happened in the area that Dalziel didn't know about. He showed up at the lake with Zenchuk and soon took over guiding for Snyder, much to the disgruntlement of Ross. Zenchuk acted as guide for the three Americans. According to Zenchuk, there was an argument, although he isn't clear as to what the argument was about.

Also, according to Zenchuk, Snyder took a photo of the 300 sheep on a nearby hill and then did everything in his power to shoot them all. He and his friends did so much killing, that it took three loaded plane trips to get all the carcasses out. One ram they shot was the largest the hunters had ever seen, and the hunter responsible was so excited he bragged that he could get half a million dollars for the trophy. Snyder, in the *Canadian Geographical Journal*, claims to have shot many black-tailed bighorn, (he probably meant Dall or stone) sheep, barren-lands-grizzly and a mountain goat, none of which, except for the mountain goat, are known to inhabit the Mackenzie Mountains.

Jim Ross wasn't happy that Dalziel had horned his way into the flow of cash coming from Snyder, but there was nothing he could do. Although it isn't clear from the interviews with Zenchuk, as best I can understand, Zenchuk says that after the hunt, he stayed with Dalziel to build a hunting lodge for Snyder and that Snyder had paid him $1,000 to do so. Dalziel then paid Zenchuk and Pete Peterson, a prospector from Yellowknife who was in the area, $10 a day for their work. But the government heard of the lodge, which didn't fit into their plans of keeping the Glacier Lake area as a game reserve, and barred Snyder from hunting in the area.

When it came time to retire, Snyder decided to fulfill his idea of becoming a "dude-wrangler." He purchased a cattle ranch in Sundre, Alberta, in 1942 and turned the management over to Jim Ross. Snyder lived there with his second wife, Louise, who had met Snyder when she was hired to nurse him after his health failed. She cured his ailments and then "did [him] the honour" of marrying him. They moved to his Bar 75 Ranch and built a mansion that Snyder called the Tepee, which was full of rare books and paintings, stuffed hunting trophies from around the world, and Dene and Inuit artifacts that he proudly displayed to all the important guests.

Snyder returned to Glacier Lake in 1952 for a third expedition, at which time he met the Yale team climbers.

The Tepee burned to the ground in 1955, and Snyder returned to the United States. He died in 1972 in Tucson, Arizona. Raymond Patterson assumed that whatever papers, photos, films, and records that survived the burning of the Tepee ended up in a Tucson museum. Not wanting to travel through the U.S., I haven't been down there to check.

LUCY AND HUGH MILLER RAUP, 1939

On June 16, 1939, Hugh Miller Raup flew into Glacier Lake with his wife, Lucy, and their two boys, David, age 6, and Carl, age 9. Hugh Raup was a professional biologist, at the lake to map the area's biological landscape for the Arnold Arboretum at Harvard University. Lucy was a lichenologist, and her collection from the area was, for reasons I never could find, heading for her garage. It was eventually donated to the Farlow Herbarium of Cryptogamic Botany at Harvard in 1978, where it was left unstudied and uncatalogued until Teuvo Ahti, a scientist at Helsinki University in Finland, examined the collection. He kept it until 1990. Then it was studied by Scott LaGreca, collections manager at Duke University in Durham, North Carolina. The latest scientist interested in the manuscript is from the University of Calgary, but to date he has not published anything on the collection.

Like Snyder and Goodwin, Hugh and Lucy had done studies around other places: Lake Athabasca (1926 and 1932), Slave River, Great Slave Lake (1927); and Wood Buffalo National Park (1928-1930). Once the kids were born, they came along on these trips. Also, there were grad students; with them at the lake was Jim Soper, a Canadian biology student who was studying under Hugh. Their contact was Snyder, whose article they had read and who had also given them a copy of the contour map made by Lambert and Stein. Snyder told them about the campsite at the head of the lake, and that he'd left some food in a cache there, plus a sectional canoe, which the Raups could use—and did.

David Raup in 1932 with a vest given to him in Hudson's Hope. Photo compliments of David Raup.

David and Carl Raup were restricted in what they could bring into the lake, and toys were not allowed. However, they knew how to amuse themselves. They would often lie in the thicket of a willow bush at the lake and carve boats with their jackknives until they had two Band-Aids on their fingers. Then the knives disappeared until the Band-Aids had completed their healing job. While waiting, they would float twigs and branches on the creek, pretending they were merchants on the Mekong or Congo River, or even, sometimes, coming up the Nahanni River. This went on until both pairs of pants were wet. Then hopefully they could take off the Band-Aids and return to whittling. The rules were simple but strictly observed. Two Band-Aids meant no knife, and two pairs of wet pants meant no playing by the water.

Carl, David, Lucy and Hugh Raup in 1939. With permission, the photo was copied at the Book and Record Depository at the University of Alberta.

While the Raups were at the lake, they circumnavigated it and, according to Soper, found the three-pole cache that was still standing and the remains of a burned-out cabin at the east end, near the creek that flowed into the Nahanni about ten kilometers farther down.

This would be the cabin that Dalziel had (maybe) flown Eppler and Mulholland into in February 1936 and also the cabin Bill Cormack had seen the following March, when he flew in with Dalziel. Later, Dalziel claimed that Cormack had looked at the cabin at Rabbitkettle Lake rather than Glacier Lake, but Cormack is adamant that he is correct.

Our information on the Raup expedition comes from the Books and Records Depository (BARD) in Edmonton, accessed when our research into park records of visitors flying to the lake led us to Hugh Raup's biography in *Who's Who in America*. This in turn led us to Hugh's son, David (famous as a palaeontologist), who was at that time still alive and had an address. He told us where his parents had donated their papers—that they wanted them in Canada, where the research had taken place. We spent a week at BARD, mining these papers and glass-plate negatives.

In 1939, when the Raups first arrived, it was common for women like Lucy to be appointed the camp cook and bottle washer. At BARD, we found pictures of Lucy cooking at Glacier Lake, in the same campground at which Snyder first settled—the one that today is used by most visitors. In the photos, though, the Raups were camped maybe fifty feet deeper into the spruce forest that surrounds the lake. In one picture, Lucy has canvas bags hanging on the trees that were filled, according to David, by him and his brother, with the water from Frost Creek that flows into the lake from the north. In the photo was also a large pot sitting on a handmade table, the legs of which were cut poplar trunks. Lucy had her head tied in a scarf as she crouched by the firepit, and she wore pants, a style that hadn't yet gained wide-spread popularity for women.

We established a correspondence with David, who took a sort of paternal interest in our research. He told us that in the late 1950s, Lucy wrote a book for campers that included a supply and equipment list for such expeditions, along with a plethora of time-tested recipes. David sent us a copy.

Lucy states that "hot cereal plays a much more important part in the camp breakfast than it does in the usual home breakfast ... and the morale of the whole day depends, in large measure on this meal." She goes on to say that the whole-wheat cereals are preferred because they taste better and because of their laxative qualities—something I had never thought of before. David, on the other hand, remembers the powdered Klim milk he had to mix every morning and claims it was a horrid substitute for the real stuff. We, on most of our camping trips, including those in the Nahanni area, use powdered milk, and I am certain that Linda Thompson, who did some of the photography for this book, can relate to David's feelings.

Lucy Raup making bread at Glacier Lake. With permission, the photo was copied at the Book and Record Depository at the University of Alberta.

But it was Lucy's cornmeal mush that came highly recommended as the best of the best. I never liked porridge much, so when we were preparing our food to take into the Nahanni, I tried the mush and decided, totally on my own, that we would not use it on our hiking trips. Lucy had also recommended frying any leftovers and eating them with syrup and/or honey—an idea that made me gag, not that hikers ever have leftovers.

On the positive side, every breakfast of Lucy's included dehydrated or canned fruit, plus bread or biscuits. We made the biscuits often and found the fat and flour fried together was finger-licking delicious.

I continued comparing the differences between the Raups and us and hoping for hints on improvements I could steal from Lucy's book. For the Raups, lunches were usually soup and cheese on bannock or biscuits. Our lunches were usually crackers with sausage (for the fat and salt) and cheese. Like us, the Raups planned their heaviest meals for dinner.

Lucy Raup making dinner on an elaborate campfire. With permission, the photo was copied at the Book and Record Depository at the University of Alberta.

The biggest difference between meal planning for Lucy and hikers like us is that Lucy based her plans on a non-moving base camp and on obtaining wild meat.

She often cooked stews, soups and the tougher meats in a heavy pot hanging on a cross-stick that could be raised and lowered over the fire so the stew could simmer but not burn. This she called a Dutch oven, and it came with a tight-fitting, concave lid that could hold coals and in turn help heat/cook the contents from the top. I have often thought of my cast-iron frying pan when camp cooking, but the weight is prohibitive, even if we used a tiny one.

Howell Martyn repairing the food cache that was used by the Raups. Note the "city" shoes. Photo probably taken by Norm Thomas and given to us by H. Martyn.

Another stove she perfected was the reflector oven to bake items such as bread, fruit pie, chocolate pie and bread pudding. A reflector oven, simple to use, has two pieces of tin/aluminum that reflect the heat from a fire onto the item being cooked. The only drawback was that she had to constantly watch it so the heat didn't fluctuate too much.

Two weeks after the Raups arrived at the lake, Lucy spotted a moose, which when shot would supplement their supply of canned and smoked meats for the rest of their stay. Hugh killed the moose, and it took them one full day to skin, cut and store the animal in their cache.

As well as animal meat, the Raups added fresh fish and birds such as ducks and grouse to their diet. Fish was quick to cook, but the birds usually had to be stuffed and roasted, which meant about an hour longer to prepare and cook.

Jim Soper, a biology student working with Hugh Raup at Glacier Lake. Photo donated by J. Soper.

Because we are always moving and don't carry rifles, we use mostly dehydrated food that has been prepared and packaged at home. This includes beef or chicken burger that needs nothing more than a bit of water and a few minutes of heat to rehydrate. As our staple, we use rice and noodles, which also cook easily over our camp propane/butane stoves or the open fire. When we fry biscuits, we mix all the measured ingredients at home and include the glob of fat inside the bag for frying in the lid of one of our pots. A bit wimpy as compared to Lucy—kneading bread while swatting bugs, often in the rain, and then concocting a form of reflected heat that would raise the bread without cooking it.

I mentioned that Lucy had the primary responsibility as camp cook, but I'm proud to say that the Canadian on the team, Jim Soper, was happy to take on a lot of the cooking responsibilities. Hugh mentions this in his journal.

"*Jim was much more of a beneficiary of Lucy's experience than me. In his journal from 1939, he mentions the desserts in words that suggest almost religious awe. He got the recipes for those desserts from Lucy and used them on his own excursions after he graduated. And, for the rest of his life, he made his own bread as she had taught him.*"

CHAPTER 11

THE PENTAGON EXPEDITION

The next visitors to the lake flew in from Watson Lake with George Dalziel in mid-June 1952 and were parts of two expeditions. First were three men who planned to make a circle north from the lake, up Frost Creek, over to and down Bologna Creek to the South Nahanni River, down the river and then up Brintnell Creek to Glacier Lake.

Watson Lake sign posts in 1944. Photo donated by Al Lewis.

Two of these men were Norm Thomas, a professional photographer from Phoenix, Arizona, and Dick Shamp, a civil servant in Washington, DC, who was an air-photo interpreter working for the U.S. Geological Survey. On this expedition, both were working for the Pentagon. Their mission was to figure out how to distinguish, on aerial photos, the creamy white coloured Cladina lichen, a.k.a. reindeer moss, from snow and to advise the military on how to move troops through that landscape. Their second job was to test U.S. military survival equipment and rations in the subarctic. But Shamp also had a personal interest: after seeing, on aerial photos, interesting fault lines near Shelf Lake just north of the Cirque and above Bologna Creek, he also intended to prospect. He carried a Geiger counter.

The third man was Howell Martyn, a Yale student hired by Shamp as a guide. Martyn, as a dedicated mountain climber, had some wilderness experience. He was the advanced column of a second expedition, the other members of which would fly in with Dalziel when he came to pick up Shamp and Thomas. They were members of the Yale Climbing Club and called themselves The Yale-Logan Expedition, after the part of the Mackenzie Mountains that includes the Cirque.

Both the Pentagon and Yale teams were partially inspired to go into the area by the aerial photos that had accompanied Colonel Harry Snyder's article in the *Canadian Geographical Journal* about his expedition to Glacier Lake in 1937. They were also inspired by a mutual contact, Hugh Bostock, of the Geological Survey of Canada. The teams had been consulting with Bostock independently, and after finding out that none of the Pentagon people had any outdoor wilderness survival experience, Bostock had advised them to hire Martyn as a guide, which they did.

At the time, the Americans were paranoid about Russians invading via the North Pole, so they built the Distant Early Warning Line (DEW Line), which was a system of radar stations across Canada's far north that ran from the Aleutian Islands in the Bering Sea to the Faroe Islands, Greenland, in the North Atlantic as well as Iceland. The purpose of the line was to detect and give early warning of a Soviet attack.

Building the Canadian section of the line involved obtaining and reading aerial photos supplied by the Royal Canadian Air Force. The problem with these photos was that the engineers couldn't decipher whether they were looking at snow or something else on the black and white images. They thought Thomas's ground level photos, put beside the aerial ones, might provide a clue.

A detailed account of what ensued once Shamp hired Martyn was compiled by Martyn's mother for family consumption; Martyn found it in his Nahanni files in 2001 and sent it to my husband, John. Martyn's mother expresses some exasperation throughout about how she had to overhear Howie's conversations with others to get the information, and when she asked for details, he wouldn't tell her anything. In my opinion, these remarks indicate that she had the true spirit of a historian. And a mother.

CHAPTER 11: THE PENTAGON EXPEDITION

She takes issue with an account that Dick Shamp gave to the *Edmonton Journal* on August 15, 1952. The reporter starts off, "It all started in 1950 when Shamp from Washington, DC, Norm Thomas of Albuquerque, and Howie Martyn, now at Yale University were attending the University of New Mexico. The three chummed together, and Shamp told the others of his plan to explore portions of the Nahanni. Both Dick and Norm had been members of a party some years ago, which planned to trek through parts of the valley but aircraft trouble cut their plans short. Norm, a writer and photographer, was interested too, and they soon convinced Howie, a botanist, to become the third member of their party."

Dudley Bolyard with Dalziel at Watson Lake, loading the plane to come into Glacier Lake. Photo donated by H. Martyn.

Mrs. Martyn remarks, "Needless to say, Howie never chummed with Shamp while attending the University of New Mexico; in fact, he never laid eyes on him until they met in Ohio, probably at Shamp's home town, in the extreme northwest, to start off for Yukon by car and trailer. Shamp had written to New Haven, to the Logan boys, asking if they had a man who could go in with him as a botanist, that he was short one man and would pay $100 plus travel expenses. The other boys from the Yale group were all set for a stretch of work in the mines of Colorado to finance their respective shares of the Yale expedition, but Howie's health didn't look good for mining. Howie's mother said that he would be anything—botanist or what have you, for $100. So, the Yale team sold him to Shamp."

Martyn says in a letter, "I was no biology student. I did a week's cramming at the Yale library so I could distinguish alder from birch and grass from sedge, and that was about the extent of my biological background."

Howie Martyn at the top of Bologna Creek, as seen from the top of Frost Creek. Thomas also called this Dog Leg River. Donated by H. Martyn.

Howie, Shamp and Thomas drove to Watson Lake. They loaded their stuff on Dalziel's plane and flew into Glacier Lake.

As soon as they arrived at the lake, Shamp, Martyn and Thomas did their three-week tour of the area. Martyn described it in a letter: "I'm a little unsure of the exact route we followed over the pass into the Bologna Creek Valley. All I remember is walking up a long medial moraine and then skirting the north slope of a ridge with a glacier or small icefield below, and then descending deeply and steeply into the Bologna Valley."

Dick Shamp on Mount Sidney Dobson, looking at the Flint Glacier. Photo donated by H. Martyn.

In another letter he says, "We followed the medial moraine up to a high, snow-filled pass, following some old animal tracks eventually down a long steep slope to the headwaters of the river that flows north west out of the major icefield that we called Flint, but that apparently is now called Brintnell. We called this river Dogleg, now Bologna, because it makes a right-angled turn about halfway to the Nahanni, entering it in a north easterly direction. The trekking along the rivers was not too bad as I recall. There are often game trails to follow and/or open gravel flats along the river edges. Some of the tributary streams were hard to cross, especially during the high-water period. The high pass over to the Dogleg River was tough, long, often steep and most of it with snow and ice."

This is Dick Shamp and Dudley Bolyard demonstrating how not to cross a creek. Photo taken by Norm Thomas, donated by H. Martyn.

As they did their planned trek, they lost their rifles, gold pans and Geiger counter, plus Shamp fractured his shoulder blade and kneecap when they crossed Bologna Creek facing sideways rather than looking upstream. By the time they reached the Nahanni, they were in poor shape and mainly in survival mode, but Thomas was still taking pictures with his large-format camera, complete with extending bellows.

CHAPTER 11: THE PENTAGON EXPEDITION   **127**

Dick Shamp makes a raft to float down the Nahanni River from Bologna Creek to Brintnell Creek. Photo by Norm Thomas, donated by H. Martyn.

The *Edmonton Journal* reported, "each carried a 75-pound pack, rifle and other small equipment and for the first few days, aside from being extremely uncomfortable, everything went according to plan. At Dogleg Creek, Dick slipped while attempting to cross and cracked a kneecap, wrenched the cartilage and fractured a shoulder blade. A few days later, he slipped again and his rifle was flung against some rocks. The rifle was damaged beyond repair."

About this, Mrs. Martyn says, "Howie says Shamp was not really badly hurt—that Shamp tends to magnify, that Shamp was a complete tenderfoot, had never been in the woods, let alone on such a trip before."

At the Nahanni, using the little rope they had left, shreds of canvas and nylon from their gear, and their shoelaces, they built a raft to float down to Brintnell Creek so they could walk back up to Glacier Lake. But the raft broke apart a few times and they lost most of their equipment, including two sleeping bags and their tent, but again, Thomas held on to his precious camera.

Dick Shamp with a large dinner to help him regain the weight he lost while going down to the Nahanni River. Photo donated by H. Martyn.

Howie says of rafting the Nahanni, "We subsequently learned that the correct way to raft the major rivers was to build small, one-man affairs that would be vaguely manoeuvrable. In our ignorance, we built a jumbo, tied together with odd pieces of rope, torn-up tent material and even a couple of shoelaces, as I recall. It was barely steerable, and we went essentially where the current took us. I remember being thrust into some rocky rapids more than once and we came to grief twice, losing much of

CHAPTER 11: THE PENTAGON EXPEDITION

our gear each time. But each time, we were able to salvage many of our logs and some of our roping. I guess it is a miracle we survived at all."

"Norm couldn't swim," he continues, "was scared and mighty unhappy about all the raft procedures. Luckily, when the raft broke up the first time, they landed on an island. Norm's perch happened to be four logs that stayed together so he rode fairly high and only half wet, but it was Howie who got the fire started—Shamp never could and Norm was too slow." Howie adds that if they hadn't found wood on that island, they would have been done for—they had no chopping tools left and anyhow were too spent to have chopped. He says he had his pack with his sleeping bag, and was keeping it afloat, hooked over the wrist that he was hanging onto the log with. He had it with him all down the river, but when he came to after hitting dry land, it was gone.

George Dalziel catching dinner for the starving explorers. Photo donated by Sherry Bradford.

The final ten miles or so up lower Brintnell Creek to base camp was stressful—otherwise they'd gotten along well. It was late in the day, and Shamp and Thomas wanted to rest, but the rain continued. They were soaked from the river and they had just one bag to sleep in and no food. Martyn had only socks and moccasins to walk in. He insisted on moving to the lake, where the food was. There was, according to Mrs. Martyn, "One brief blow-up" at the point when Shamp and Thomas thought they might be lost and were going too high and would have to go down to the lake.

When they finally got back to Glacier Lake, Shamp had lost forty pounds. They shared the one sleeping bag they had left and ate army rations. Impatiently, they waited a full week before Dalziel picked them up.

He arrived in mid-July. There are various accounts of what happened next, but it seems Dalziel came in empty or with a pile of Yale equipment. Dalziel, after seeing the starving men, hauled out his fishing equipment and fed them. Either that night or the next morning, he flew Shamp and Thomas out, while Martyn waited another day. Dalziel returned with the Yale team.

Back in the States, Thomas wrote *"Man Against the North,"* a story he intended to sell to a famous magazine. Martyn was assigned to market the story but didn't know how, so it remained unpublished until 2002, when it was published in *Diary of a Lake*. Thomas's photos were used in Shamp's published report, which mainly dealt with soldiers choosing routes through the area. The report on the survival equipment indicated that it was the food that got them through the three-week journey to the Nahanni River and back to Glacier Lake.

Martyn's report on the vegetation came late; Mrs. Martyn mentioned Shamp "Pressing for his (Howie's) botanical notes. Howie claims there were only four kinds of trees that he could see, but he isn't sure that he could always tell them apart. That report should be a honey!" And Howie himself wrote that, "Frankly, it's not very interesting."

CHAPTER 12

TUNGSTEN TO GLACIER LAKE HIKE 1999

It was the story of Dalziel and the missing trappers, Mulholland and Eppler, that took us into Glacier Lake and the Cirque of the Unclimbables in the summer of 1999. We wanted to poke around the burned cabin, if we could find it.

By this time, John had put together his research on Dalziel and Snyder and on Dick Turner, Bill Eppler, Joe Mulholland and other trappers along the Liard and Flat Rivers. This was the main incentive that led us to the lake and Cirque. But we were after the whole story of how these men occupied the area and what happened to the ones who lived, as well as the ones who died.

On this hike there was no attempt to reach the Nahanni overland from Tungsten, although we knew that if we took the time and carried enough food, we could easily have walked the trail from Glacier Lake to the river, a well-trodden trail used by river rats on the South Nahanni who want to come up for a close look at the Cirque. Some guided tours of the river include this hike.

The most likely route for us was not up Zenchuck Creek, as we'd assumed a few years before, but up Kuskula Creek, which flowed into the Rabbitkettle just below the pass where we'd been with Shea Walsh. Kuskula Creek was shorter, though it involved crossing the Flat River just above Tungsten. But we found little information about this route.

There were two young fellows from Oregon who claimed to have walked from the Cirque to Tungsten by crossing the Brintnell Glacier. They said it took them two days—urgent days, because they had missed their flight out of Glacier Lake and were short on food. We didn't believe them. The glacier is crevassed and dangerous, especially in summer.

John and I put a team together that consisted of us, Carol Fairhurst and Richard Lazenby, both living in Prince George; Elzebeth Vingborg from Denmark, who had gone to Howard's Pass and Union Carbide with us; and Stephan Biedermann from Germany, whom we had met and hiked with many times in Kluane and who was young, strong and capable. And we had Michael King, an animal-psychology student from Toronto. He had been in Kluane with Stephan and hiked with us there, and what he lacked in experience he made up for in enthusiasm.

Our route, we figured, would take around fifteen to eighteen days if we had no problems. We chose a departure date plus time to get to Tungsten, and booked a pick-up date from Glacier Lake for eighteen days after we crossed the Flat River just out of Tungsten. Jacques Harvey (rather than George Dalziel) of Simpson Air (now Wolverine Air) made a date to take us back to the Flat Lakes. We would piggyback onto a return flight he had scheduled for the Moose Ponds. He would do a little side trip by landing at Glacier Lake and flying us to the Flat Lakes. This turned out to be financially beneficial to everyone.

Our eighteen days allowed for the six obstacles, according to the map, that could turn us back. The first was getting across the Flat River. If we couldn't ford the river, we would have to adjust our plans and go up Zenchuk Creek, but that, as we knew, was a tough bushwhack and not what we wanted, especially with our heavy packs weighted down with tons of food for six people for eighteen days.

Our second obstacle was the 30 kilometers of bushwhacking we'd have to slog through going down the Rabbitkettle River. We calculated that we could do a maximum speed of one kilometer per hour, which would take us three days to complete, and it would be our toughest section. Our third obstacle was a canyon on the Rabbitkettle that could stop us dead. Walking through a canyon was usually not possible due to water lapping at the canyon walls, and walking up and over the adjacent hills looked steep and difficult, according to the contour lines. The fourth obstacle was to ascend the even steeper hill out of the Rabbitkettle valley and up onto a valley rimmed by Mount Sidney Dobson to the east and what was left of the Flint Glacier to the west. We knew we'd have to do this early in the morning when we were fresh—if we could do it at all.

Getting onto Mount Ida would be easy if we managed to get into this valley. The map indicated that getting off Ida could be done by following a rock glacier down to Brintnell Creek.

Our final obstacle would be crossing Brintnell Creek so as to be on the correct side of the lake, ready for pick-up. The map showed a braided washout area below the canyon on Brintnell where we could possibly cross. A report on the Internet claimed that just above the washout was a tree across the canyon where people could shimmy across. This was the other possibility, but we suspected that this information was posted by the two guys who also thought they could get from the Cirque to Tungsten in two days.

Our trip up the Nahanni Range Road was uneventful. At the washout we saw a pickup truck and, on the other side, another pickup. Then we saw a grader crossing the creek, as if there was nothing there.

It was Gerald and Terri Pitt and the kids, heading to town.

"Want a ride across?" he asked.

We loaded bikes and gear into the bucket, and I climbed in beside Gerald while the rest stood on the running boards and held onto the bouncing loader as we sailed across the raging water. Gerald crossed again and left the loader by the washout, waved to us and climbed into his truck.

Bikes, gear and a few hikers take the easy route across the washout.

That night at the Flat Lakes cabin, we drank the wine we'd brought with us. The following morning, we were lined up for a photo along the road down to Tungsten, at a spot that looked best for starting our bushwhack down to the Flat River.

Steph's pack weighed in at 75 pounds, the heaviest of them all, and Carol's was close to 50 pounds, which was half her body weight. We needed our poles to keep ourselves from falling over. Everyone else was at about 60 pounds.

Elsebeth, John, Rich, Steph, Mike, Carol and Viv, with heavy packs, ready to go.

Steph takes Mike across the fast-flowing Flat River.

CHAPTER 12: TUNGSTEN TO GLACIER LAKE HIKE 1999 **137**

Crossing the Flat River turned out to be as difficult as we imagined. Steph, being the strongest, crossed at a section that looked fairly flat and wide. Flat means the water is lower and the current gentler. He succeeded and then came back to take Mike across; Mike followed in Steph's wake. When we saw their success, we did the same, with the weaker people crossing in the wake of stronger ones. Once we were safely across, we trekked uphill through a forest with little undergrowth.

John at the Mirror Lake cabin.

The shore around Mirror Lake was muskeg, so we climbed high to get around it and soon came across a cabin with a good, solid roof but walls partly chewed by porcupines. John was ecstatic. We set up camp. The rain started. Then Mike decided he wanted to go back. His knee was bothering him. He had done some fancy wheeling with his bike on the way in, scrambling through ditches and the up side of slopes.

We repartitioned the meals and snacks, and John and Steph walked Mike back to the river, where Steph took him across, making this Steph's fifth crossing of the day. Mike planned to spend the next eighteen days fishing at the Flat Lakes and maybe visiting/helping the caretakers at Tungsten.

While waiting for Steph and John to return, we huddled around the wood heater in the cabin. Elsebeth cut firewood and Richard hauled water. But the day was passing quickly, so we started making supper. I imagined John and Steph shepherding Mike all the way back to the cabin, making him dinner and putting him to bed. But they turned up just as supper was ready.

Crossing the rock slide at the end of Mirror Lake.

The following morning, the sun came out and we hiked along the side of Mirror Lake, over a boulder field created by an old slide and then up Kuskula Creek. As the sun climbed higher, we put creek-crossing shoes on and walked through the freezing water. With each foot of elevation gain we could see back across the valley, where the Nahanni Range Road curved down the mountain from the pass, appearing as a tiny scar squiggling along the side of the hill.

Fed by two glaciers, Kuskula Creek offered clear, cold water for drinking and plenty of flat camping spots on the gravel washouts, plus a waterfall that we had often admired through binoculars from the road. We spent our second night on one of those washouts and the third in the bush, near the pass leading to the Rabbitkettle River.

We put our sandals on and walked up Kuskula Creek. It was easier than side-hill gouging.

On the morning of the fourth day, we spotted the Rabbitkettle River valley, with its thick cover of spruce forest cut in a few spots by the meandering river. We became silent. The forest looked impenetrable. I dared not point my camera at anyone in our group for fear of a mutiny. We started the bushwhack down, in single file, through vegetation so thick that each person was unseen three feet in front of the next.

An hour later we did an easy crossing of the Rabbitkettle River, not far from where Shea, John and I had turned around to head back down Zenchuk Creek a few years before.

The canyon on the Rabbitkettle River we weren't sure we could get around.

We rested at the side of the Rabbitkettle. I changed my socks. Carol had a chocolate bar. Elsebeth needed another pee. Steph wanted a coffee. John wanted to go up to the pass for a nostalgic look. We stalled, looking at the sun, the mountains, the trees, the creek. Finally, we could stall no more. Richard threw his pack on his back and headed into the bush. Usually soft-spoken and not excitable, he let out a "yippee" like I'd never heard before. What we hadn't factored into our plans was that, because the upper Rabbitkettle valley was narrow, there was a distinct animal trail that looked like a groomed walkway, similar to what you'd find in a park. Even if it lasted for only a kilometer, we thought, it would help.

The animal trail continued and continued and continued. Even in those times when we had to relocate it, when it deviated off to some side-trail, the main path was never far away. We were ecstatic.

The following day, our fifth, we reached the canyon and our third possible obstacle. We could see that there was no way of going around the base, as the river's main channel licked the sides of both walls. We found that bushwhacking through thick alder was the only possibility. The animal trail had fanned out to at least twenty paths, none of which went up, with some dead-ending in swamp. But we managed, within a few hours, to cross above the canyon and descend to the river again on the other side. We had just three possible obstacles left.

The Rabbitkettle valley opened up, and we could walk on wide, treeless riverbanks or on gravel and sand riverbed as easily as walking down a country lane. That night, the camping was on flat ground, the fire was fed by an endless supply of dry driftwood, the sun was shining and the creek flowing, into the river from above, was clear.

In celebration, we finished our first plastic mickey of whiskey. John wrote a cryptic note that included our names and phone number, rolled it up and pushed it into the bottle, and sent it afloat to, he hoped, the Nahanni River, the Liard, the Mackenzie and finally the Arctic Ocean. No reply has ever been received.

Early the next afternoon, we arrived at the base of Mount Sidney Dobson and spent the afternoon in a grassy spot by a tiny creek, reading, writing, washing clothes and generally relaxing in anticipation of our steep climb in the morning. If we couldn't make the climb due to a bluff or cliff, we would continue down the Rabbitkettle to the hot springs. We didn't want to retrace our steps, and we figured if we got to the hot springs, there would be a warden who would be able to put us in contact with our pilot.

Walking on the "Appian Way" in the Sidney Dobson valley.

The ascent onto Sidney Dobson took about six hours, with Elsebeth being the only one who fell. Her injury was minor and Band-Aids stopped the bleeding. Once on top, we were relieved to be on almost flat ground again and that there were just two possible obstacles left. We thought we'd probably make our destination. At least, judging by the maps, we would see it. We camped at the foot of a small hanging glacier. Carol and I hadn't had enough climbing for the day, so we headed up again to a spot that provided even better photographs.

Sidney Dobson valley is what the Yale team called the south fork of the Fool's River. It offered a walkway paved with small flat stones that looked to us like Italy's Appian Way. Some of Dobson's peaks were with ice and others with jagged ledges, and we passed close to a second hanging glacier that fed a blue alpine lake.

At the far end of the valley, on the side of a hill covered in blue lupins, we stopped to have lunch. After kicking off our boots, we scattered our pack contents around the hill and luxuriated under the blue sky.

Forty-five minutes later, as we swung left, to the northwest and toward Mount Ida, Richard noticed a sow grizzly with her cub walking directly ahead of us in the narrow valley that led upward. I noticed the wind blowing our scent away, so she didn't detect us. We jumped over the creek, climbed the side hill and watched as she sauntered down the valley, nipping flowers and digging marmot holes with her cub always nearby. She grazed for a moment directly beneath us and then started working back up the valley, exactly where we wanted to go. We called. She stopped dead and sniffed the air, her nose pointed in our direction. At that same moment, the cub scurried between her front legs. She sniffed again, we shouted and then the two bolted up the opposite hill, the cub just in front and above her. They disappeared within seconds. We named them Sid and Ida, after the mountains we were on.

That night, camped in the shade of Ida near the top of the creek, we were relieved that Sid and Ida never came to visit. The following morning, after a leisurely breakfast, and just as John and I huffed up over the last bluff, Steph, usually reserved and calm, came running down the hill, hollering, "It doesn't matter in which direction you look, it's the most beautiful place on Earth!"

And once on top, we agreed. Mount Proboscis, in all its unique majesty, was across the valley that separates Ida and the Cirque, showing off its broad front wall. The peak of Ida was to our right, and it looked like an easy walk to the summit. The Brintnell Glacier was blinking white ice to our left, and behind us in the distance were the peaks of Sidney Dobson.

After an hour of gawking, photographing, and bellowing about the beauty, reality took hold and we tried to figure out a route off Ida. The rock glacier on the map turned out to be a hanging ice glacier with blue compacted ice and deep crevasses. We'd have needed ropes and crampons to descend. We guessed that this was what the Yale team called the Split Glacier and the route down was what they called Split Glacier Pass. The steepness of the slope near the hanging glacier didn't allow us to see very far down, so choosing a route was chancy. At this point, John wanted to return to Tungsten and sit in the hot tub with Mike. We ignored him and chose to descend the steep scree north of the hanging glacier, just as the Yale team had done half a century before.

Richard and Carol descending the steep scree slope of Mount Ida.

Sure-footed, Richard was part way down, with Carol right behind, when he came to a ledge from where we had to lower our packs with a rope. While standing on the ledge with the packs lined up, someone accidentally knocked Carol's pack over and it bounced down, hit the ground, bounced again in a higher trajectory, hit the ground again and bounced a third time, in an even bigger orbit, before crashing near the bottom. We stood silent.

"I'm glad no one was attached to that," Richard finally mumbled, and everyone expelled a sigh of relief.

With even more caution now, we picked our way down the slope to Carol's pack, which was resting on a moraine that led down to Brintnell Creek. The pack was okay, but the pepper spray, still encased in its side-pouch, had exploded. We buried it under a cairn.

In the distance is the washout on Brintnell Creek where we crossed.

It was twelve hours after we broke camp in the morning that we arrived at Brintnell Creek and stopped on the gravel washout. We were far too tired to attempt a river crossing, so we made camp, had a quick dinner and hit the hay.

The following morning, under dark skies and before breakfast, we packed up and crossed Brintnell with little difficulty. The cold temperature had slowed the glacier's melting and lowered the level of the water. We were all but home, our six obstacles behind us. We made camp on the washout and had breakfast with a second cup of coffee. While sipping silently, we looked up the slope of Mount Ida, now covered in snow. Lots of snow. That snow would have made it impossible to descend, had it come one day earlier. It also meant that there was no way back.

The log over Brintnell Creek that was considered crossable by those posting on the web.

I remembered the climbers who claimed to have crossed on a log hanging over Brintnell and said that they made their way up and across the Brintnell Glacier. We explored the creek to the canyon above the braided washout we'd crossed in the morning. A tree lay across the canyon, just as the fellows on the Internet claimed.

The log was about 25 feet above the raging, boiling water and was a good 20 feet across and 2 feet in diameter at the butt. It must have washed down the creek at high water and lodged itself there.

And yes, some climbers with proper gear might have been able to shimmy across the log, but it wouldn't have been any of us! Especially with heavy packs.

As we poked around, we found some climbing rope on the ground, but it was frayed and old, probably left about ten years before.

The following day, under sunny skies, we descended Brintnell Creek for a couple of hours and arrived just below the face of Cathedral Mountain, at the entrance to the Cirque. Above us whole sheets of granite hung, just waiting to crash down. We slowly climbed the talus, with rocks the size of pickup trucks, some of them tippy, like they'd just fallen. Finally, we reached Fairy Meadow with flat ground.

And just as we hit the area of hobbit rocks, where tents could be struck under outcroppings for protection from the weather, we were met with rain, the first we'd seen in fourteen days. In the meadow, we talked to climbers, three groups from Europe and Asia who had waited for thirty-two days for the weather to clear enough to get a day's climb in. They talked mostly about the various food drops they had. One story featured a powdered cappuccino canister hitting the rocky ground and exploding.

The following morning, it was still raining, so we headed down to Glacier Lake. As a way of exploring, we split up, with John and me going through the trees while the rest went back down the talus. We agreed to meet at the climber's trail that ran diagonally across the mountain and above Brintnell Creek. We bushwhacked through the forest, where the trees were sparse and the floor was covered in soft moss. Walking was easy. We came to a bridge that crossed the creek flowing from the meadow and stopped to wait for the rest. They arrived about twenty minutes later.

At the lake, we found thirty-seven other humans, the most we'd seen in two weeks.

"It feels like New York City!" said Carol.

CHAPTER 13

THE YALE TEAM

It would be nice to think that the first person to climb in the Cirque was Fred Lambert, the conqueror (I wonder about that word when it comes to mountains) of Mount Logan but there are no actual records or details about this climb.

It was Bill Clark who said that George Roberts, another Fort Simpson trapper hired as a boatman on Snyder's 1937 expedition, climbed Cathedral with Lambert.

Lambert, in his *Alpine Journal* report, never directly mentions going into the Cirque. He says, "Of the seven triangulation stations established, five were climbed twice, our highest climbs being 5,000 feet above the lake. The triangulation points also constitute camera stations … ." He goes on to say that the expedition arrived at the lake on July 15 and that a week later, July 21, Mr. and Mrs. Snyder flew out to meet Lord Tweedsmuir at Eldorado Mine and they took George Roberts with them.

So, Roberts was there for only a week. If Cathedral was climbed in order to set up a triangulation station, it is more likely this was done by Lambert and a fellow climber from New York by the name of Stein. But it is even more likely they wouldn't have used Cathedral at all, because lugging a camera up a sheer face wouldn't be easy, especially with the climbing gear they had in those days. Howell Martyn, in a letter of May 2001, said, "I find it very unlikely that Roberts and/or Lambert climbed Cathedral in 1937. It is a formidable peak, and I think they would have memorialized its ascent in more detail than they did."

But again, the lake sits at 2,585 feet and the summit of Cathedral is around 8,000 feet, so they might have done it.

Credit for the first climb in the Cirque went to the five Yale students who were members of the Yale Mountaineering Club. They climbed Cathedral for sure but reported arriving at a false summit.

As far as the Yale team knew, when they arrived in 1952, they were entering virgin ground where no other climbers had been. The leader of the group, Dudley Bolyard, said in a letter, "To my knowledge there had been no serious previous attempts to climb these mountains. We saw no cairns or other evidence of prior ascents."

It was June when the Yale climbers arrived at Glacier Lake. Howell Martyn, still burnt out, no doubt from his experience as a Pentagon employee, but rested, even if starved for a week, stood on shore and watched as his climbing friends, Dudley Bolyard, John Christian Bailar III, George Yntema, and Harry Nance landed on the lake. They had flown in with Dalziel when Dick Shamp and Norm Thomas from the Pentagon group flew out.

The following account of their time at the Cirque and surrounding mountains is taken mostly from Bolyard's self-published book, *Living on the Brink*, 1998, with supplementary material from Martyn and Martyn's intrepid mother.

Dudley Bolyard camping on a glacier in 1952. Photo donated by H. Martyn.

Martyn and Dudley Bolyard were roommates at Yale University in Connecticut and members of the Yale Mountaineering Club. After reading Snyder's article, Bolyard contacted Dr. Hugh Bostock, of the Geological Survey of Canada, about the article and photographs. Bolyard said, "His report contained photos of mountains and we ascertained that none of them had ever been climbed." Martyn said in a letter of October 2000, "In 1952 my room-mate at Yale, Dudley Bolyard and I, active mountaineers, became intrigued by the chain of mountains known as the Mackenzies about which little then was known, at least in mountaineering circles. A variety of inquiries ultimately put us in touch with Hugh Bostock of the Canadian Geological Service in Ottawa. Hugh became a friend and supporter and identified several areas in the Mackenzies that were intriguing. Of these we picked the area around Glacier Lake, the mountains of which were called the Logans."

Besides climbing, Bolyard planned on writing his master's thesis about the geography of the area between the Rabbitkettle River and Glacier Lake—largely the Sidney Dobson massif and the glaciers between the

Brintnell Glacier and Dobson. I suspect they did most of their climbs on Dobson, just because that was their leader's focus.

They then solicited John Christian Bailar III, a Yale medical student, and George Yntema, a physics student from Yale. After hearing about the trip, Harry Nance, a graduate in philosophy who went to the University of Colorado, asked to be part of the team and the rest quickly accepted the offer. Nance had climbed numerous peaks in the US with Bolyard, so his skills had been tested and approved. What made Nance a bit different was that, due to an accident in the chemistry lab in high school, he had lost part of his right hand, including the thumb. His belaying techniques were creative rather than the tried-and-true methods of most climbers.

As Martyn put it, "We put together a five-man team and called ourselves the 'Yale-Logan Expedition.' Four of us were Yalies, and the fifth, Harry Nance, was from the University of Colorado. In the spring of 1952, we learned that another party was visiting the same area and needed a third man. That put us in touch with Dick Shamp and eventually I was nominated to join the Shamp expedition. This reduced our costs by 20 percent. And this left Bolyard to do all the dirty work of organizing the Yale-Logan Expedition."

Bailar, an adept hobby photographer, had a large-format (4-by-5-inch) camera and offered to provide pictures for the team's use. Martyn may have also had a camera.

After selecting the team, what remained was the raising of funds to pay for the flight in, gas for the car to get to Watson Lake, and incidentals. The Yale Mountaineering Club was the official sponsor, but the trip was expensive and Bolyard's team needed more money than that offered by the club. They worked diligently, obtaining donations and raising sponsors for equipment and supplies in exchange for endorsing the products in advertisements. Martyn had accepted the job of guiding for Shamp and Thomas from the Pentagon team, for which he received $100. Martyn went in a couple of weeks earlier than the rest of the Yale fellows, at the expense of the Pentagon team.

George Yntema, 1952. Photo donated by D. R. Flook.

Like the Pentagon team, the Yale guys headed north pulling a tiny travel trailer filled with gear and supplies. They pulled it behind Yntema's 1952 Chev and drove the Alaska Highway to Watson Lake. After a few delays due to engine trouble with Dalziel's plane—trouble that Dalziel adeptly fixed—they flew into Glacier Lake and settled themselves at the east end, near the burnt-out cabin and remaining bear cache. Martyn said there was no sign of any cabin but that he had already fixed up the cache to be used by both teams.

The majestic Cathedral Mountain, rising straight up several thousand feet above the lake, constantly drew their attention, but they left exploring it until later. Bolyard's thesis must have been a deciding factor.

They named and ascended several peaks, all parts of or close to Sydney Dobson—Fang, Marble Mountain, Plymouth Peak and Snow Chute—and they explored ice fields, taking exceptional care not to fall. Near the edge of one icefield, they shot a caribou and Bailar showed his anatomy skills by directing the butchering. Like the Raups earlier, they needed the fresh meat, and also like the Raups, they jerked as much of it as they could.

The rugged Mackenzie Mountains were enticing to climbers in the 1950s.

Nance and Bolyard then climbed a peak they called Red Wing, named after the boots that had been donated to them. They roped up and followed a steep gully to the summit, sat and had lunch in the sun, and then started down, but Bolyard soon realized that the conditions had changed and the snow wouldn't hold them. At one point he stepped over to the left to what looked like a safe ridge. Nance decided to continue down the main route, and within a moment was tumbling down, with a huge mass of wet snow sliding with him. He hit a boulder at the end, but luckily didn't suffer any broken bones. They continued belaying each other down the challenging mountain until they reached a dangerous ridge. Darkness was almost upon them, so rather than chance a serious fall, they tucked in for the night. In the morning, they resumed their descent and reached the valley floor within a few hours.

The following day, they looked at a circular mass of ice that covered the upper third of what they called Ice Dome Peak, located south of Red Wing. Viewed from the west, the mountain appeared to be an interesting but not a hazardous climb, for the glacier itself sloped away from the summit at a 20-degree angle and the rock below was a mixture of easy cliffs, buttresses, ledges and dotted with small areas of talus. Viewed from the north, however, the mountain presented an entirely different aspect. It appeared to have been split, as if by some titanic axe, with one side falling completely away, so as to produce a topographic and geologic cross section. Bolyard's examination through field glasses revealed no crevasses on the glacier.

Bailer, Yntema and Bolyard climbed Ice Dome Peak from the easier western side. Soon after emerging onto the glacier, they roped together, reluctantly, because it slowed their progress. But they soon encountered crevasses, each marked by a narrow strip of white snow, which contrasted with the slightly grayer snow that had not yet been compressed. The lead climber tested each crevasse by plunging his ice axe through the snow. Invariably the snow would be only six to 10 inches thick, and underlain by a solid substrate of ice, indicating that the crevasses were closed.

Three-quarters of the way up the glacier, they came to a different kind of crevasse. The whiter snow was wider. Bolyard eased his way to the edge of the crevasse, probing with each step. Suddenly, his ice axe fell through the snow all the way to the top of the shaft. He then probed about a foot farther and found thin ice. While Bailer and Yntema belayed, Bolyard leaned as far out as he could, probed again, and found solid ice. He then took a short run to gain momentum and sprang through the air as far as he could. The ice collapsed under his weight and he fell into a lake of icy water about 35 feet below.

The ice leads to a glacier—possibly the one Bolyard fell into. Photo donated by H. Martyn.

He knew he was in trouble if he didn't do something quickly. Looking around, he spotted a ledge about 10 feet above the water. His crampons were the 12-point variety, with sharp chisel points protruding horizontally, which enabled him to climb onto the ledge.

After reaching safety, he looked around and found that he was in a large cavern with overhanging walls and no obvious way out. Looking up, he saw his rope leading through a small hole in the snow. Being struck by the beauty of the greenish blue ice, he yelled up to Bailer and Yntema for a camera. After taking two or three photographs, he then set about figuring how to climb out of the crevasse.

The only way was to make a rope stepladder. He pulled two short ropes out of his pack and attached them to the main rope by a prussic knot, one that could slide upward but, when weight was put on it, couldn't slide back down. He would use these two sling ropes as stirrups and work his way upward. Yntema and Bailer, located on the far side of the crevasse, fixed the belay rope, but Bolyard had to swing out above the lake like a pendulum before he could start climbing upward. However, theory and reality were often quite different. In this case, the ropes were smooth nylon and wet so they didn't hold. His only solution was to once again lower himself into the freezing lake so he could pull himself straight up the rope and onto the ice above.

By this time, Bolyard was shivering. He climbed hand over hand up the rope. A second rope was dropped down to belay him. But the friction of the rope had cut through the wedge-shaped lip of ice near the top and he couldn't reach the hole. And he was shivering uncontrollably by now. Bailer leaned over the hole, grabbed Bolyard by his belt and gave a mighty tug. Bolyard scrambled out of the ice hole and landed on the surface of the glacier, panting.

Luckily, they had a primus stove and some Cream of Wheat with them. Even before Bolyard sat up, Bailer started the stove and cooked the cereal, which warmed the inside of Bolyard's shaking body. Once back in New York, Bailer and Bolyard contacted the company that made the cereal and told them the story. Bolyard was interviewed about it on a popular radio program called *Grand Central Station*.

In his book, Bolyard wrote, "The Ice Dome Peak experience is not one that I would ever wish to repeat or recommend to others. I did not seek the experience, and I certainly did not enjoy it. For some time, I tried to drive it from my mind, but before long I came to realize that fear was not part of the experience. Confidence and determination were the dominant emotions; and, together with the persistence displayed by my companions, were responsible for my survival."

The team went up Cathedral too, late in the season, in September. They camped on the 14th at the base of the mountain and on the 15th, they woke to snow. They climbed on the 15th and according to Bolyard, "The climb was easier than expected and we made the summit shortly after one o'clock. Upon reaching the top, it was clear that we were on the wrong mountain and that Cathedral massive is divided into two distinct peaks by an ice-covered col."

In the course of that climb, it started to snow, and it continued. They realized that they were tired, so rather than try to hit the big peak they descended to the lake to wait for pick-up. While waiting, they heard a clap of thunder and watched a piece of the face of Cathedral collapse.

Mrs. Martyn had some things to say about her son's adventures with the Yale team. About how the group got along, she says, "I think the group of five were not too well assorted; two wanted a more dudified kind of life and couldn't be got going early enough to make the top of some of the climbs they set out on, even with the long daylight hours. But at least they never came to out-and-out blows—I guess it may have been close on a couple of occasions. By the end of their stay, so much new snow had fallen on the mountains that they weren't able to even take a try at the best and biggest of them. The ones they had been saving for their pièce de résistance. They were badly held up getting flown out by bad weather—and by the time they were all out at Watson Lake, there was two feet of snow. At that, they had to leave all their gear back at the camp, and Bolyard waited until the pilot could get back in and pick it up. By the time he left, on the 9th of September, full winter had come."

That story has date discrepancies; the team arrived at the lake in June. They were apparently in there for seven weeks. The team claims to have climbed Cathedral in mid-September and then waited until the weather cleared at the lake before they were picked up. Mrs. Martyn has the team leaving on September 9, which would make the time in there a minimum of nine weeks. However, Flook (see chapter 14) says that the Yale team went up Cathedral on August 14, and he kept a journal, so August is probably the correct date.

Mrs. Martyn also mentioned that the food must have been okay because Howie gained back what he'd lost with the Pentagon team plus another 15 pounds. She finished by saying, "He wants to go back!"

Like Lambert, the Yale team didn't register their climbs, but once they returned to the States, Dudley Bolyard published an account of the Yale team climbs in the *Canadian Alpine Journal*, #36 (1953), and then in 1998 he self-published the book *Living on the Brink*, with a chapter, "*Controlling Fear*," that is a good account of his seven weeks with the Yale team in the Cirque, including the two excerpts quoted above. During all that time and due to difficult terrain and bad weather, they managed to climb just nine peaks, plus they explored part way up and down the Rabbitkettle River. Bolyard said that after climbing in the area, the "most promising and desirable areas lie north of the Flat River and south of the Rabbitkettle." He was referring to Mount Nirvana, which was later crowned the highest mountain in the Northwest Territories, rather than Mount Sir James McBrien, located near the Cirque.

Mount Sir James McBrien was thought to be the highest in the NWT until Nirvana was proved to be higher.

CHAPTER 14

WINTER RESEARCH

Our list of flights into what became Nahanni National Park included references to the guest list for Snyder's last visit. On the list was D. R. Flook, of the Canadian Wildlife Service, which then had an office in Fort Simpson. We checked the usual sources: the National Museum that had a deal with Snyder to collect certain specimens, the National Archives; and the Earth Sciences Information Centre. The first sent a list of pamphlets and articles by Flook and had nothing on another member of the expedition, a Dr. H. Jennings.

As it turned out, George W. Scotter, an ornithologist who did preparatory work in establishing the park, knew Flook personally and provided his address. As well, Scotter advised us to contact the Canadian Wildlife Service in Edmonton to see if Flook's reports were available, as well as any reports by Flook's successor at the Edmonton office (the

Fort Simpson office was shut down), R. C. Stewart. Stewart covered the Liard/Nahanni but was there only for a couple of months before leaving for Agriculture Canada.

We got Flook's two reports, from both him and Canadian Wildlife Service. The first, "Snyder expedition, 1952," contains a daily journal from August 2 to August 29, 1952, and a list of wildlife observations. The second, "Marten in the central Mackenzie region/season, 1952-3" contains a journal, March 23-26, describing visits with chief warden W. Day and old Nahanni hand Gus Kraus as guide. It is this report that describes the situation with Yukon poachers coming into the Flat River watershed. This reference clued me into what Dalziel and his assistant Cormack and Zenchuk had been up to.

In letters, Flook clarified some of the information Snyder, in his 1937 article, had provided on game animals.

SNYDER RETURNS WITH FLOOK

Flook and Snyder came in while the Yale team were climbing on the glaciers up Brintnell Creek. With Flook and Snyder was Snyder's second wife, Louise, plus two American hunting buddies. Snyder was there to collect caribou specimens for the National Museum. Maybe because they were starting to get suspicious of Snyder, the Canadian Wildlife Service assigned Flook to watch over him. Flook was the first biologist to file a report to the Canadian Wildlife Service about the wildlife around Glacier Lake.

In a letter of March 13, 2000, Flook filled us in on the situation: "I was the first and last Canadian Wildlife Service biologist at Fort Simpson, but there were game wardens before and after me and at least one Northwest Territories biologist, Hugh Monaghan, a few years later. My appointment and terms of reference made no mention of the Nahanni and most of my attention was devoted to the Mackenzie lowlands, where almost all native hunting and trapping took place."

D.R. Flook with Gus Kraus. Photo compliments of Flook.

Men securing a rope to help ferry a dinghy full of gear back and forth. Photo donated by H. Martyn.

CHAPTER 14: WINTER RESEARCH

Flook mostly stayed in camp, recording his wildlife observations. This included observations of Snyder and friends.

On the evening of August 12, shortly after the Snyder party arrived, Bailer and Yntema appeared at the west end of the lake, across from Snyder's camp. Flook paddled over and interviewed them about the wildlife they'd seen and learned that the three had been on the Brintnell Glacier. Flook then took them back across the lake, where they borrowed Snyder's collapsible dinghy and hauled the gear from the cache at the east end of the lake up to Snyder's camp at the west end.

Howell Martyn on Frost Creek—note the canvass backpack. Photo donated by H. Martyn.

Wanting to see the Brintnell Glacier up close, Flook then helped the climbers carry their gear to a gravel flood plain at the foot of the glacier. From there, Flook hiked up the northwest side of Mount Ida, followed the next day by a hike five miles up Brintnell Creek to the toe of the glacier. They all returned to the lake late on the 13th, and Flook took a photo of Yntema and Bailar at Snyder's camp. It was on the 14th of August that the Yale climbers left for Cathedral.

Flook remained near the lake and hiked up the slope north of the lake and west of Frost Creek to the 5,500-foot elevation level, but preferred the area up the eastern side of Frost Creek. He went up the east side to avoid a hanging valley and then returned to the creek bed near the creek's source.

Flook returned for more studies the following year, and over the next couple of decades the Canadian Wildlife Service continued to employ him. Prominent among the officers involved with Flook was George Scotter, who made three trips to the lake altogether, in 1970, 1971 and 1974. On one of these trips, he was accompanied by a CBC film crew led by Garnet Anthony. The pictures taken at Glacier Lake were lost due to a faulty camera.

In his letters, Flook elaborated on various events that weren't connected to his wildlife reporting. He says on August 29, the day they left, "An associated Airways Belanca piloted by Ron Page from Hay River flew in to pick up Glen Kilgour and me from Glacier Lake. The rest of Snyder's party had already been flown out to Fort Simpson. En route, the airplane picked up Ollie Rollog, Slim Raider (old-timers with some experience in the region) and David Aonica from Virginia Falls and deposited them at Glacier Lake. They had been flown from Whitehorse in June by Dalziel Airways and had walked and paddled an improvised canoe to Virginia Falls."

Flook wrote to us about other expeditions with Gus Kraus and sent photos of Kraus and his circle at Nahanni Butte.

MODERN SCIENTISTS: DONALEE DECK

After the Nahanni area had been studied by scientists and the findings recorded, the attraction of the place for scientific study declined. The mountains had been measured and photographed, the vegetation had been collected and recorded, the animals counted and studied. The glacial melt was calculated and daily temperatures were documented. Climbers became the next big group of explorers of the Logan Mountains.

Climbers were the next group of explorers to the Cirque of the Unclimbables.

That was, until an enthusiastic anthropologist working for Parks took interest in the area around Kraus Hot Springs, located below First Canyon on the South Nahanni. This quickly led her to reading about what the earlier scientists had found around Glacier Lake.

The anthropologist, Donalee Deck, had earned a degree in anthropology from the University of Regina in 1985, before going on to obtain a master's degree from the University of Manitoba. Her master's thesis was on wood charcoal remains from the Lockport site, located beside St. Andrews Dam just out of Winnipeg. Although the anthropologists there were mainly looking for artifacts to shed light on early European pioneers, they also found bone tools from as far back as 1200 A.D.

After graduation, Deck's curiosity in Canadian heritage, especially the Aboriginal part of that heritage, was piqued during a field trip to the Gilmore site in Saskatchewan, where she saw first-hand evidence of people living on the Canadian prairies before the arrival of Europeans. Each summer, Deck worked at different sites in North America and eventually became an assistant for the Saskatchewan Research Council for the Nipawin Dam Heritage Study.

For the next few years, Deck worked in Manitoba, but in 1990-91 she volunteered for the Canadian Parks Service to survey in Grasslands National Park in Saskatchewan. Then she went north to help salvage the excavation of an umiak (an open boat made of skin) in northern Yukon. She followed this up by working at the Herschel Site in Saskatchewan, a 1,500-year-old Aboriginal ceremonial location.

I am certain the knowledge Deck obtained from studying the Aboriginal sites contributed to her becoming the Archaeologist for Parks Canada in 2006. She was assigned to work in the Indigenous Affairs and Cultural Heritage branch. Deck then worked in Cypress Hills, at Riding Mountain National Park, and in 2008 at the Kraus Hot Springs and Poole-Field-cabin site in Nahanni National Park. For her, getting a project in the Nahanni area was a grand stroke of luck.

I found out about Deck's work in the spring of 2019, when Stephan Biedermann, one of the hikers who walked with us from Tungsten to Glacier Lake in 1999, drew my attention to a newspaper clipping about a new anthropological discovery at the Cirque of the Unclimbables. Deck was the anthropologist mentioned in the article, and when I tracked her down, she sent me the park's summary of her research:

A pre-contact site was discovered during archaeological testing in 2012 at Fairy Meadows in the Cirque of the Unclimbables. The site was located at the base of Mount Huey directly north of Mount Harrison Smith. This corresponds to the entrance of one of the finger valleys in the Cirque.

The pre-contact artifacts included a broken stone tool, likely used as a cutting implement, a core and flakes from stone tool production. The artifacts were located in an organic black layer extending between 8 and 17 centimeters below surface that also contained charcoal. The organic deposit with the artifacts was AMS (Accelerator Mass Spectrometry) dated to 1970 years ago.

According to ethnographic research done by Catherine McClellan and reported in her book, *My Old People Say*, a map indicates that the Mountain and Kaska First Nations people lived in the area of the South Nahanni, Liard and Mackenzie rivers. McClellan says the trader Poole Field, a North West Mounted Police officer from Dawson City who had established the post at Nahanni Butte in 1924 and operated it until 1935, reported that these people fought each other in the late 19th century. I assume these people had lived here long before the arrival of Europeans and could have enjoyed the Cirque as much as we do today.

As well as her findings in the Cirque, at Glacier Lake, Deck found evidence of people being at the campsite at the west end of the lake. There were nails in trees from which the Raups, Snyder or even Brintnell possibly hung water bags or pants to dry. Or maybe the nails were put there by the early climbers. The growth around the nails would indicate the timeframe of when they were pounded into the tree.

Deck also found evidence of a food cache that was possibly the same one repaired by Howell Martyn (see photo on page 124.) Deck also found the foundation of an old cabin, possibly the one that was still standing, according to George Cormack, when he flew into Glacier Lake with Dalziel while they were looking for Eppler and Mulholland. But I'm speculating. A more detailed report will be available in the future.

At the time of writing, Deck was working out of Rabbitkettle Lake during the summers, and part of her study includes impact assessments. When she was in the Cirque and around Glacier Lake, she was not only awed by the beauty of the area but also impressed with the care the climbers had taken of the land. The climbing pitons were sparse and hardly visible, tucked deep in the fissures of the rocks. But most important, there was no garbage or equipment left around the Hobbit Rocks, where the bored climbers waited for good weather for days on end. In her view, the area had been "well respected by climbers."

CHAPTER 15

THE CLIMBING RUSH

Three years after the Yale team was flown out of Glacier Lake by Dalziel in September 1952, the Cirque of the Unclimbables started seeing the next group of Americans, climbing enthusiasts, and recreationalists who reported on the four, small, parallel cirques, which include a dozen vertical granite walls of about 800–1,000 meters each, topping out at about 2,500 meters in elevation.

These enthusiasts, all highly experienced climbers, were Arnold Wexler, Donald Hubbard, Ray D'Arcy, Dave Bernays and Sterling Hendricks.

Wexler, an American born in 1918, tested climbing ropes and equipment for the military during World War II. He made over 100 ascents, 50 of which were first ascents, before he came to Canada. He had a reputation for climbing in uncharted territory, especially if the climb presented an exceptional challenge. He knew he'd find that in Canada.

Donald Hubbard was much younger. Born in 1939, he is credited with finding an inscription, "D.B. September 16, 1908" that had been left on Seneca Rocks, a group of razorback ridges in West Virginia that are the only inaccessible peaks in the states, except for climbers using technical rock-climbing techniques. The inscription is assumed to have been made by D. Bittenger, a civil engineer surveying the area for the National Park Service.

Ray D'Arcy was a student at MIT and had scaled and recorded numerous new routes in New Hampshire before moving to Yosemite, where the famous El Capitan, the twin rock to the Cirque's Lotus Flower Tower, is located. At El Capitan, D'Arcy is known for encouraging climbers to find new and safer routes than those originally recorded.

Dave Bernays, born in 1932, became an expert climber who also improved the necessary hardware that climbers use. His snow picket, at the time of his death in 1980, was still considered the best design ever.

Sterling Hendricks was born in 1902 and accomplished at least 50 first ascents, mostly in the U.S. His most notable event came in 1957, when he was climbing with Don Hubbard and Rex Gibson in the Bulkley Range near Smithers, B.C. Gibson fell, pulling the other two down with him. Hendricks was unhurt and ran miles to the town's hospital looking for help, but it was two days before he returned, and by then Gibson had died.

These five climbers flew into Glacier Lake on July 2, 1955, with Dalziel. According to Wexler, "The view of the Logans (Ragged Range) first from the air and then from the ground, was an exhilarating experience. In spite of the forewarning by Lambert and Bolyard we had not anticipated the ruggedness that confronted us."

"The peaks rise out of this amphitheatre in bleak, black, smooth faces," said Wexler. "Even with careful scrutiny through field glasses we could discern no obvious approaches to the summits. The rock was unrelenting in its high angle and unbroken expanse. The peaks forming the second amphitheatre were equally bulwarked with sheer faces. All we did was look and then retreat to camp."

But they felt compelled to climb Cathedral (Harrison Smith), which formed the southern wall of the first amphitheatre. As they stood on the summit, they had a good look at the surrounding peaks, and it was these peaks that gave Wexler the idea of calling the area by its foreboding name. It was his proclamation of the peaks being unclimbable that, in turn, enticed members of the climbing world to face the challenge themselves.

The team left Fairy Meadow three days after climbing Cathedral and returned to Glacier Lake on the pretext of getting more food. "I suspect that part of our haste in leaving was the feeling of frustration engendered by these peaks with their sheer faces of flawless granite. They looked impregnable and impossible."

Rather than going up Cathedral again, they moved up Brintnell Creek toward the Brintnell Glacier and climbed the canyons at the upper end of the creek and, for a time, on the surrounding glaciers. Upon return, they camped in Fairy Meadow, near the stream beside Cathedral, and again climbed it using two different routes. They also ascended numerous other peaks in the surrounding amphitheatres. But none of the peaks had names at the time, so it is difficult to decipher which peaks they climbed. I am sure the lure of Lotus Flower Tower and Proboscis would not have been ignored.

Five years after Wexler's expedition, Bill Buckingham, an enthusiastic American climber, spent a month conquering most of the highest points in the Cirque, including the south ridge of Mount Proboscis. Its southern face looks like it has been cut in half, revealing a polished granite tower that goes 2,000 feet straight up. Although it looks deceptively easy, according to Buckingham, once in line with the upward direction, it is horrifying. The mountain has a 24-pitch route with seven pitches graded at 5.12, and this route is considered the easiest free-route choice. This mountain remains one of the most difficult summits in North America.

Mount Nirvana, located in Hole-in-the-Wall Valley, is the highest mountain in the NWT.

While Buckingham was enjoying the views from Mount Proboscis, John Milton and Ed Arnold had landed at Hole-in-the-Wall Lake, located between the Flat and Rabbitkettle Rivers some 30 kilometers to the south. They were there to do some ecological research and climb for fun. Milton was on Mount Savage and could see Mount Nirvana from its summit. He reported this information at a later date to Buckingham, who returned to the area three years later with climber Lew Surdam. They were the first to climb Nirvana. After approaching it from the south, which they decided was too steep, they went to the northwest ridge on the mountain and successfully scaled the peak. They also established that Nirvana is actually the highest mountain in the Northwest Territories, rather than Mount Sir James McBrien, as was previously thought.

Mount Sir James McBrien is at the top left, and a ridge from McBrien leads to Lotus Flower Tower. At that time, McBrien was thought to be the highest in the NWT. Photo donated by H. Martyn.

Royal Robbins, in 1963 was fascinated by Yosemite's Half Dome. Physically almost the same as Proboscis, Half Dome had never been conquered until 1957. Robbins, Mike Sherrick and Jerry Gallwas managed the first ascent of Half Dome's Northwest Face, the first successful Grade VI climb ever completed in the United States. Six years later, Robbins, along with Dick McCracken, Jim McCarthy and Layton Kor, hung from the southeast face of Proboscis.

Climbing routes were shared, and eventually, the climbing community decided that Lotus Flower Tower rather than Proboscis was the most challenging climb in the Cirque. Although Buckingham climbed Lotus first, in 1960, he did it by traversing along a ridge that connects the Lotus Flower Tower with Mount Sir James McBrien. Its 2,200-foot southeast buttress of solid granite, similar in scale and elevation to Half Dome, is

CHAPTER 15: THE CLIMBING RUSH

the wall that gave Lotus its reputation, and it wasn't conquered until 1968. It is Harthon Bill, Tom Frost and James McCarthy who get the credit for being the first up that wall. In recent times, the Lotus Flower Tower has been popularized in the book, *Fifty Classic Climbs in North America*, and is described as "one of the most aesthetically beautiful rock faces in the world."

The Lotus Flower Tower's southeast buttress has twenty pitches, with each pitch being 60 meters. At the end of ten pitches, which usually takes climbers a full day to complete, the wall has a mossy ledge big enough to hold a tent. This means that climbers don't have to hang by ropes in a bivouac to get some rest. The second half of the climb, according to renowned climber George Bell, has "nearly a thousand feet above and below, marred only by vertical cracks extending its entire height." Bell also states that there are xenoliths (rock fragments embedded in the larger rock when the magma of the larger rock was cooling) dotting the wall, which are perfect hand holds, making the entire rock equivalent to an indoor climbing wall.

CHAPTER 16

A NEW PARK

The Dene people are believed to have used the area for around 9,000-10,000 years. One reason people could live here during the last ice age, the Wisconsin Age (85,000-10,000 years ago), is that a strip of land that bordered the Nahanni River was never glaciated, so people could pass through.

Nahanni National Park earned park status in 1972, after Prime Minister Pierre Elliot Trudeau paddled a portion of the river and was inspired by its grandeur. Once back in Ottawa, he had 4,766 square kilometers of land placed into reserve, and four years later the area was officially declared a national park reserve. It remained so until land claims agreements were settled in 1978, when it got full park status.

Then, in 1987, the river earned Canadian Heritage River status. The Nahanni Butte Dene Band, Dehcho First Nations and Parks formed a committee in 2000 to prepare a memorandum of understanding for the expansion of the park. They agreed that the new boundary would cover 30,050 square kilometres, which included the Cirque of the Unclimbables and Glacier Lake, the Flat River and the Little Nahanni River. The expansion excluded the Flat Lakes and Tungsten. To the south, the boundary would reach Skinboat Lakes, the upper reaches of the Caribou, Mary and Meilleur Rivers, plus the Tlogotsho Plateau and Hole-in-the-Wall valley.

After the expanded park boundaries were announced in 2009, the park received full approval from the United Nations and became a UNESCO preserve.

How the park officials decided where to place the expanded boundaries is a long story. It started, as best I could discover, with a 1971 report written by George W. Scotter for the Canadian Wildlife Service in Edmonton. Scotter was the recipient of the prestigious Douglas H. Pimlott Award that honours those who have contributed to "Canada's biodiversity, landscapes and wilderness."

After studies conducted by Scotter, Norman M. Simmons and Hilah L. Simmons from Fort Smith, and Stephen C. Zoltai from the Canadian Forestry Service (also in Edmonton), the experts strongly recommended that the boundaries of the new park should include Hole-in-the-Wall and Glacier Lake. Over a period of less than ten years, Scotter published an additional fifteen articles about the area, many with recommendations for preservation of land and wildlife.

Scotter felt "The development-fever prevalent in the Northwest Territories today will make it difficult to give even the area within the originally proposed boundaries National Park status." He went on to explain that the rich mineral and hydroelectric power resources could easily trump the idea of a "wild rivers" park, as the Park Service recommended in their report of 1970. Scotter went on to point out some of the hot springs in the region and the historical log cabins dotting the area that could become tourist attractions and/or campsites. Being a biologist, he collected thousands of plant specimens to be catalogued and studied at a later date, and he pointed out that some of these plants were rare and needed protection.

He also identified, among a herd of six animals, the first dark-phase ram (Ovis dalli) ever seen in the Mackenzie District, specifically at Howard's Pass. His report on the birds, published in 1985, indicated that there were forty-one rare and fifty-seven uncommon species living in the park, with some of those having breeding ranges within the area.

With the idea of the park expanding its boundaries, John L Weaver, a renowned conservation biologist, headed a study between 2002 and 2005 on the distribution of large animals within the suggested new boundaries of the park. He found that wolverine, moose, black and grizzly bears, Dall's sheep, caribou and mountain goats were all present in healthy numbers and remarked that to remain healthy and flourish, they needed large areas free from hunting and from industrial activities like oil, gas, mineral and hydro exploitation.

Weaver's report weighed in heavily for the expansion of the park, which resulted in more studies being conducted. One such report by the United Nations Environment Programme and the World Conservation Monitoring Centre, in 2011, discussed the richness of the flora in the expanded park. They stated that 700 species of vascular plants and 325 bryophytes were identified and that 42 species of mammals, including beaver, grey wolf, wolverine, lynx, woodland caribou, moose, white-tailed deer, mountain goat, and Dall's sheep made the area their home. A wide range of rodents plus two endangered myotis bat species were also part of this ecosystem. A total of 180 species of birds were identified, which included the peregrine falcon, the golden eagle and the trumpeter swan in limited numbers. Sixteen species of fish commonly found in the streams flowing into the Flat and Nahanni Rivers were also identified.

After more studies were completed, specifically on the woodland caribou, because they were of socioeconomic importance to the local First Nations people, Weaver found that hunting and predation were the greatest threat to the caribou, and that roads needed for industrial purposes would give humans easier access and increase this threat. He also reported that a popular calving area was near or along the territorial divide (Howard's Pass area) and the Little Nahanni River. Calving is a time when the young are most vulnerable, and caribou usually spend from June to September grazing in these areas so the calves can strengthen before the rutting period starts at the end of September, when moms aren't quite as protective. After the rutting period, fall and winter migrations start and include the Hole-in-the-Wall area and passage along the Flat River. If industrial pollution destroys existing plant species or introduces invasive species of plants that would change the food supply in these areas, this too would endanger the survival of the caribou.

Caribou often use small glaciers and icefields for protection from insects. The Brintnell – Bologna Icefields in the Ragged Range hold the two largest glaciers in the park, totaling about 30 square kilometers of ice. Besides these, numerous smaller glaciers are present in places that are shaded from the sun or have substantial snow deposit; these are often accessible to caribou. But, in the last 26 years of improved observation methods, which now use satellite images, scientists have found that these glaciers had decreased in size by 30%. For example, in 1952, most of the area to the west of Mount Sidney Dobson (a pass that leads from the Rabbitkettle River to Glacier Lake) was observed, by geologist Dudley Bolyard, to be glaciated with solid ice from the Brintnell Glacier almost to Sidney Dobson. He called it the Flint Glacier. But, as I discovered when I crossed this pass in 1999, the Flint has now entirely disappeared.

During hot summer weather caribou use the remaining icefields and small ice patches for relief from insects such as the mosquito and bot fly. Large swarms of mosquitoes like those present in the lower, wetter areas of places like Lened Creek, can kill a caribou calf by entering through the nose thus causing asphyxiation, and bot flies nest and distribute their eggs under a caribou's skin, which cause severe parasitic infections that are lethal to the caribou.

For those of us travelling in these areas using contour maps, we found the disappearance of icefields and glaciers impressive. When we compared photos of the Brintnell Glacier taken by the Raups in the '30s, by us in

1999 and then again by me in 2015, it is frightening to see the extent of the disappearance.

More recently, biologists working for the Department of Resources, Wildlife & Economic Development, claimed that when they observed the caribou in the Selwin Mountain area and the northern part of the Ragged Range, which includes Glacier Lake, they counted about 781 caribou. From this they estimated the entire herd to be 940 – 1140 animals. The research also found that, when the Tungsten mine was operating, the herd was stressed and numbers decreased due to low calf survival.

When we look at the history of hunters, trappers and recreationalists who haunted this area for the last hundred years, we can see that the reported numbers could be correct. For example, the early trappers, after harvesting all the available animals along the Liard River, went into the Flat and Nahanni area. Albert Faille trapped along the Flat for many years, and the Flying Trapper, George Dalziel, placed numerous men on his own lines at Zenchuk Creek, the South Nahanni near Rabbitkettle Hot Springs, and Glacier and Rabbitkettle Lake until he was legislated out of business in 1937 by an act of parliament. Their take was up to $7000 for a winter's catch of marten and fisher pelts when marten was worth $50 each and a fisher was around $30. And this size of take was repeated often, until the entire area was closed to white trappers. In the course of about 20 years, large areas of the South Nahanni drainage were stripped of marten.

Today, entry to the park for most recreationalists is expensive due to the area's isolation. When I did the river in 1984, the cost of flying into Rabbitkettle Lake with Simpson Air was around $1000 for two canoeists and one boat, and day-trippers often flew to Virginia Falls for an afternoon. Those who joined a tour group paid up to $500 per person, per week for a guided trip down the river.

In 2019, the cost for three people to fly from Fort Simpson to Glacier Lake, where the entrance to the Cirque of the Unclimbables is located, is $2,600, and a fly-over is $630 per person with a minimum of two people. For two people and a canoe to fly from Fort Simpson to the

Moose Ponds at the headwaters of the South Nahanni and near Mount Wilson is $2,855, and a guided trip is anywhere from $7,300 to $9,500 per person, depending on which trip is chosen. This is not a cheap three-week vacation. Flying into Glacier Lake from Finlayson Lake with Kluane Air is $2,000 each way for four people and is the most popular option climbers use to access the Cirque.

If entering the park from the west, at Tungsten, which is accessible most of the year by 4 X 4 and is close to the headwaters of the Flat and the Little Nahanni Rivers, or if flying in from Findlayson Lake to Glacier Lake, total trip costs can be reduced. But this also makes it easier for poachers, hunters and those with back country vehicles to enter the area.

As a result of our earlier visits, we proposed in 2000 that the park be expanded to include the Flat River. We were glad to see that happen, but as is always the case with enthusiasts, the realization of our dream by the Canadian government caused problems that we should have foreseen. Now, to go to the park from Tungsten, the Flat Lakes, or the road to Howard's Pass, we have to pay to hike a whopping annual sum of $165 each. As soon as we leave the Flat Lakes in an easterly direction, we are in the park, not heading for it. Also, we have to abide by whatever rules the park establishes. Finally, what happens to all that interesting junk that John loved so much? Parks usually burn junk and cabins, in case idiot recreationalists like him sometimes hurt themselves.

One such place threatened is the mill site on the east side of the Flat and just out of Tungsten, where some canoeists, we noticed, had sheltered after a late start, using the coffee table to make some adjustment on their splash covers. The Mirror Lake cabin, where we were so comfortable for a night during our hike to the Cirque, is another. There are also remains of exploration sites around Glacier Lake and a cabin above Lened Creek with the roof caved in but with the deck still comfortable. Those are just the ones we found, and I am sure there are others.

CHAPTER 17

GLACIER LAKE/ CIRQUE 2015

P lans for my return to the Cirque of the Unclimbables started like all my trips, in mid-winter, at dinners when a fire crackled in the fireplace and wine flowed into glasses. This is a time when memories of discomfort, pain and even danger are buffered by the atmosphere. But most of my friends know what I'm up to. I'm recruiting. They are wary. Not unreceptive, totally, just wary.

One cozy evening, with all the necessary items (fire, food, wine) in attendance, my friend Linda Thompson, a skilled hiker and photographer, suggested that we fly into Glacier Lake. Years before, she had started hiking after seeing my slide show about the hike from Tungsten to Glacier Lake.

"We can take cameras and equipment and even a bit of wine," she reasoned. "If we hike in like you did, we'd have to carry really heavy packs full of food."

I argued a bit about flying in, since the walk from Tungsten is spectacular and I wasn't sure if the granite monoliths would be as impressive without the labour of getting there. But as I thought about it, I realized that Linda had a great idea. Fifteen years ago, I was just plus 50. Now, (you do the math) the idea of hiking with less than sixty pounds in my pack is irresistible. And the idea of returning to the Cirque had its alluring charm. It would be a way of seeing if any changes had happened after the expansion of the park.

So, Linda and I planned for a fly-in and three weeks of hiking. I couldn't be happier to have her as my co-conspirator. Linda had been in Kluane National Park with me the year before, walking to the Donjek Glacier, and we were accustomed to each other's eccentricities. When I suggested that a certain pass would be a "cakewalk," for example, she knew what I meant and checked the maps and the landscape carefully for alternate routes.

Our next question was "how many?" Under the Cirque's difficult conditions, six people would be best—enough for safety should someone get hurt, yet not so many as to make decisions complicated. The question after that was, "who?"

John was out. He'd had a hip replacement and preferred to avoid heavy packs and walking for eight hours a day for weeks on end. He considered flying in and hanging out at the campsite, maybe going down the lake and locating the elusive burned cabin. "Maybe," was his answer, which really meant "not likely."

We had a short list of potential candidates. Deb Hazell had been with us in Kluane the previous year and survived almost unscathed—Deb and I had had an unplanned swim in the Duke River. According to Linda, Deb's confidence in me hadn't been shattered in the least. Maybe just cracked a bit. And she was strong enough to carry seventy-five pounds up extremely steep slopes at a pace faster than I could manage with just half that amount of gear. We were also accustomed to each other's quirks and quarrels.

Peggy Tobin, a notoriously strong hiker who had done numerous week-long hikes with the local hiking club, was our next candidate. She had also heard me reference "The Cirque Hike" often, comparing it to hikes in our vicinity. The stories had intrigued her. On yet another wine-inspired winter night, when we mentioned the possibility of going in, her instant response was, "I'm in!"

That made us a team of four. We needed two more. An obvious one was yet another member of our Kluane team, Vancouver resident, Kelley Faubion, whom I'd met a few years before in Chile, where we had done a difficult hike up a still erupting volcano. She and her partner Hash Goonetilleke, who had also been in Kluane with us, would be great.

More wine, in Vancouver this time, at Marcello's on the Drive. But Kelley hesitated. She'd let me know, she said. Hash remained silent. I called. I emailed. I wondered, "What the hell?"

But our plans continued to include them. In April, I went to Vancouver again, and Kelley and Hash met me for breakfast rather than the usual dinner. Hmmmm, I wondered.

"I'm pregnant," she said, with the largest smile I'd ever seen.

"So, I guess your pack belt won't fit by July."

Hash smiled, too. If he was like John, he was thinking, "Got out of that hike in an innovative way!"

Although disappointed about their absence on the trip, I congratulated them on the great news of yet another hiker entering this world.

But now it was Linda, Deb and Peg sitting around the fire with me, filled wine glasses in hand. We decided we'd go with four.

After booking a flight, cooking and dehydrating meals and packing, we drove the Stewart Cassiar Highway in northern B.C. to Watson Lake and then up the Robert Campbell Highway in Yukon to Finlayson Lake, where we expected to be picked up by Kluane Air's fixed-wing Beaver plane.

Kluane Air's fixed-wing Beaver that flew us into Glacier Lake.

Hoping to get out the same afternoon as we'd arrived at Finlayson, we stood on the dock, our "all inclusive" vacation packs at our feet, and watched the yellow and brown plane land. But it wasn't for us. Cam Sutcliff, the pilot, took some Brits who had arrived after us to a lodge on a lake an hour away. The following eight hours or so were quiet and we slept in our tents in the gravel parking lot by the lake.

Early the following morning, we heard the plane again and rushed down to the dock. Cam couldn't take us to the Cirque yet because he had to transport Americans staying at the lodge to some hot fishing spots. He was there just to refuel.

He flew off and within three hours was back again. This time, he dropped off an assistant who fired up one of the derelict trucks that was parked in the gravel pit and loaded it with empty propane containers. The assistant was heading into Watson Lake to refill the containers and would need a plane pick-up when he returned four or five hours later.

We couldn't go to the Cirque while Cam waited. He had to go back to the lodge and take a fisher to Whitehorse so he could catch his plane back to the States. Neither of these destinations were in the direction of the Cirque.

Resigned to the fact that we weren't flying soon, we sat reading and sucking up the sun. That soon became boring, so we walked the dusty road to a lookout point two kilometers uphill. We explored a creek that crossed the road until the bushwhacking became unpleasant, and then we returned to the gravel pit for lunch. Finally, we took our packed gear to the dock and then checked out a First Nation hunting camp, complete with abandoned cabins, that was just half a kilometer from the landing dock. Once back at the gravel pit, we tapped our toes and Peggy sang tunes from the 1960s. I was impressed that she remembered every word of every song and was able to keep a tune.

"I hear something!" Linda shouted, interrupting the music. We froze. Sure enough, we could hear the now familiar drone of the plane's engine as it approached the lake. We raced to the dock and waited, cheering its arrival. Cam confirmed that it was finally our turn to fly.

But Cam seemed to stall. He checked the fuel barrels up at the gravel pit and he had a snack. He refuelled the plane and cleaned out the back seat, where the fishers had left some garbage. He offered to take photos of us, and he looked at our maps to see what we had in mind as hikers.

We realized that it was only our sense of urgency that made Cam seem hesitant to take off. Cam was just relaxed and careful.

Finally, we loaded our packs and ourselves. Since it was the first time Peggy had been in the area, we put her in the front so she could get a bird's eye view of the terrain.

Cam told us that, due to the clear skies, we'd be able to fly over the Brintnell Glacier, circle the Cirque and approach the lake from the east. This was a lucky break; we could see the area before we walked it, and we could take photos. We lifted above Finlayson Lake and started across the tundra. It looked inviting and nonthreatening from where we were, but, in reality, walking that bog would take all one's energy to go a mile, plus all one's blood to feed the mosquitos that lay in wait.

Then the mountains came into view and, as we soared above, I peered at the rugged and isolated landscape. A story Warren LaFave, owner of Kluane Air, had told me when I booked the flight, came to mind. A few years prior, Warren had been at a conference in Oregon and met up with two guys who planned on walking from Tungsten into the Cirque, a distance of 75 kilometers of off-trail hiking. They believed they could do it in two days. No matter how much Warren tried to tell them this was not possible, they knew better.

The following summer, Warren happened to be flying climbers in his helicopter over the Rabbitkettle River about a kilometer from its source, and below where our team had crossed. He noticed two fellows on the bank of the river waving wildly for his attention. Suspecting it was the two guys from Oregon, he left them waving and flew over the Brintnell Glacier to deliver his passengers into the Cirque.

An hour or two later, he returned and landed. Sure enough, it was the two fellows from Oregon. They were wet and miserable and, because the water was so wild, they were unable to cross, which they had to do to get to the Cirque.

"The pass where it begins is just a kilometer up-valley," Warren told them, pointing. "No problem hopping over the trickle up there. Then you could go down river for a couple of days, up onto Mount Sidney Dobson and over to Brintnell Creek. That'd take you just over a week."

But the boys had had enough. They agreed to pay Warren for a lift back to Tungsten. This country was too wild for them. Once I heard this story, I suspected they were also the ones who posted on the web about a two-day hike that crossed the Brintnell Glacier and down the glacier's outflow to the base of the Cirque. Warren didn't say that these guys were climbers, though. If they were, they would have been lugging a ton of rope and equipment. Anyway, that posting, with dangerous information, has since been taken off the Internet.

As we flew, we could see the Flat River and Flat Lakes below and where the mountains loomed in every direction. Then I noticed a new road snaking above the Little Nahanni River. When I asked, Cam told me that it was a new mining road that ran from Tungsten to Macmillan Pass and that a small section of the road is tucked inside the park's new boundaries.

"Need to carry gas if you're on that road," Cam said. "It hooks up with the Canol Road, and then you've got to go south to Ross River, where you can get gas at an inflated price."

"I thought the road stopped at Howard's Pass," I said, but got no response.

Within minutes of flying over and between other ice-capped mountain peaks, I realized that most creeks, valleys and pinnacles had never felt a human boot. The mineral distribution lent shades of red, yellow and brown to the rock, and the upper valleys were fed by melting glaciers. I kept peering down, thinking how much I'd like to visit each and every valley we passed.

"Holy shit," I muttered as we crossed an exceptionally rugged spot, the speaker of my headphone on full blast.

"No more of that," Cam said.

I assumed he was religious, and I could understand that anyone who flew bush planes over this country would want to be on good terms with God. I swore no more.

We crossed over the Brintnell Glacier, its crevasses threatening even from the plane. The granite peaks in the Cirque came into view. We circled once and flew to the east end of the lake. As we dropped, the immense monolith of Cathedral Mountain guarding the entrance to the Cirque loomed ahead.

"Oh, my fucking god!" Peggy hollered, her body leaning forward, her hands gripping the dash. And then her hand came up and slapped against her mouth. I heard Cam chuckle, so I figured he'd given up worrying about God now that we were landing.

Cathedral Mountain reflected in Glacier Lake. Photo by Linda Thompson.

We hit the lake with hardly a bounce and taxied to the gravel bar where the outfitters had built a small, windowless plywood cabin that could provide shelter in an emergency. This was where most climbers left gear that couldn't be carried up to the Cirque on their first trip.

I jumped down and introduced myself to those standing on shore. They were park officials who had been doing campsite work and were waiting for their own pick-up. They knew we were coming in by the park permits we'd acquired, and they had picked up my name. As Linda, Deb and Peg disembarked, the park officials whooped and hollered a warm welcome.

Peggy smiled for just a second and then walked to the edge of the lake and stared at Cathedral, her mouth agape.

"Next week, you can touch it, Peggy," I said. "If you have any strength left after you've climbed up Frost Creek and back."

"Personally," I said to my group of gawkers and the park officials as we stood around the lake, "I like the name *Cathedral* better than *Harry Smith*."

Linda agreed.

FROST CREEK HIKE

With coffee cups in hand, we stood with our backs to Cathedral, watching mist slowly rise off the lake, listening to our music—the creek gushing water down the rocks and through the Frost Creek canyon.

Within an hour, we were dressed, packed and ready to bushwhack up the hill to the mineralized Red Mountain named by Snyder over eighty years ago.

We had a rough idea what we were in for. The best description of the route was by Norm Thomas, the photographer on the Pentagon team. We had some photos, but over all, they were ambiguous. Shamp and Martyn standing in shoulder-high bush staring at Mount Sir James McBrien. Martyn striding through bald alpine. Shamp and Martyn staring down a precipitous boulder and a shale-strewn slope into the valley of Bologna Creek. And, in all his pictures, heavy overcast.

His story made it a little clearer, at least concerning our climb up to alpine. We wouldn't make it far down Bologna, which Thomas describes as a typical creek-walk with constant boulder hopping and crossings of tributary creeks or the main creek when it encountered a bluff.

Thomas says this: "Going through the spruce forest along the north shore of the lake, sizeable trees but growing out of slide substratum so there was lots of windfall and large, mossy irregular boulders underfoot. Down low on the slopes and in the bottoms along the streams we had dense spruce forests with jumbled windfalls and deep moss, and where there were little streams or swales, there would be impenetrable thickets of willow and alder that grew so thick that a man, many times, couldn't push his way through."

Thomas continues, "Higher up on the mountain sides the forests disappeared, but dwarf birch grew about shoulder high and thick as a meadow. It tangled around your legs until you couldn't move ahead and sometimes, it threw you down."

And higher still? "The mountains were awfully steep and there were dangerous slide areas and treacherous rocks overgrown with slippery moss so that you could not see the holes between the rocks until you had already stepped in them and fallen through. There, too, were snowfields with rotten crusts so that you could almost walk over but you never quite crossed one that you didn't suddenly drop through up to your waist and then had to struggle out, dragging your pack behind you."

Thomas also records them deviating off, near the top, in search for a way over to the headwaters of Bologna Creek, into a canyon, and had to go back and try again, this time successfully.

Obviously, he wasn't having much fun, and this was written long after, in retrospect, which in my case always results in a kind of golden glow, a mellowing of memory, to the point that I can actually say to people, "That one was a cakewalk."

We'd be up, too, where Lucy Raup had taken her boys, Carl and David, collecting lichens. We had seen a photo of the family eating lunch in that dwarf birch that Thomas mentions, with Glacier Lake far below. Our other source, Donald Flook, hadn't mentioned the bush at all, just the animal sightings and the bear scats and moose pellets. Must be nice to be a biologist and happy in an impenetrable jungle.

We hiked along the lake about a kilometer east of the creek, where our map indicated a gentle hill. Our first hour was through birch forest with almost no underbrush except for the high-bush cranberries that were ripe and tart. I remembered that Ida Snyder had stayed in camp one day and picked cranberries (she called them currants) from these same bushes.

With each hundred feet of elevation gain, the hill became steeper but still not difficult.

Lucy and David Raup collecting lichen near Glacier Lake. With permission, the photo was copied at the Book and Record Depository at the University of Alberta.

Another hour, and the willow and alder replaced the birch. Deb, standing over six feet, was swallowed up by the trees, and the only way we'd see her was when she pushed the alder aside and held it firmly so we could pass. The sun was out and we could smell the steam rising from the forest floor.

"Let's try to hit the creek!" I yelled, after about three hours of battling the bush.

"Stay level and we'll hit it!"

The bush got thicker and the walk more difficult.

"What if we spring a bear?"

"No respectable bear would be in here."

"That's not what Flook said."

CHAPTER 17: GLACIER LAKE/CIRQUE 2015

Deb Hazell and Peggy Tobin sipping cool water from the creek and anticipating the push through the thick brush to the alpine. Photo by Linda Thompson.

Finally, we arrived at the creek. It was wild and the bush grew right to its shore. There was no going upstream along any washouts. We had lunch, drank litres of clear, cold water, and headed back into the willow. Deb and Peggy disappeared within three steps. Linda kept calling to make sure she wasn't lost.

Peggy found an animal track and we followed it, but lost it again within minutes. Our uphill struggle kept on and I was starving. Finally, the alder shrank into scrub birch that rose only to our shoulders. We kept ascending, and the walking became easier. But it was well past time to make camp. We were exhausted.

Then Peggy, in the lead, stopped and gazed around.

"That's home!" I called when I saw she was standing in an opening. We gathered beside a trickling creek with surrounding swamp, what Thomas had called a swale. I found a dry mound slightly smaller than my tent, but it was the only dry spot. Luckily our tents were waterproof and kept the sopping ground from leaking in. During the night I heard the thumping of heavy feet. I sat straight up and listened. The thumping stopped and then started again, but soon disappeared.

"You okay?" I got grunting responses.

The bright morning sun woke us, and after breakfast we started walking and found an underground spring that bubbled above a welcoming pool. It was so strange and unexpected that we stopped to see if we could find a feeder spring, but had no luck.

Pool being fed by an underground spring.

"This'd make a good place to camp," I said after about two hours of trudging.

"We've only been walking for two hours," Deb said, tapping her watch.

My friends humoured me, let me eat and drink, and encouraged me to keep going.

"This'd make a nice campsite," I said shortly after, pointing to a flat spot on the alpine carpet.

"You said that ten minutes ago!" Deb yelled. This was something I'd never heard her do before. She must be tired, I thought.

I trudged on. Peggy went ahead and disappeared over a small knoll.

"The lake! The lake!" she called.

"Our base camp," I sighed with relief.

We pitched tents and secured the tarp. My friends headed out to a beckoning ridge while I "guarded" the tents. I lay under the tarp, and watched their colourful dots on the hillside disappear. George Goodwin, a bilologist who had come to Glacier Lake in the summer of 1937 with the Snyder expedition, had been collecting small animals for study and climbed up to the lake under Red Mountain, where I was presently resting. He had seen goats on the ridges above the lake and the skeleton of two moose with their horns locked together in the lake.

Lake at Red Mountain at the top end of Frost Creek.

The following day we went even higher, behind Red Mountain, toward a second lake and what we hoped would be a manageable pass. Once in the valley, I took one look at the gigantic rocks that seemed to have just landed days before and said, "Nope, not for me."

But Peg and Deb wanted to circumnavigate the lake by climbing on the boulders around its shore. While waiting, Linda and I bouldered at the entrance to the valley.

Peg and Deb returned three hours later. Both were shivering. Deb told us, "At the far end, I was trying to get past a huge rock. I had one leg over a crevasse and my arms gripping the rock in front of me. The rock I was holding moved and my extended leg slipped. I crashed to my knee. When I looked down into the abyss, I knew, one mistake and I'd fall, probably to my death. I have never been that scared before. Once I regained my balance, we went back a few rocks and then down to the lake. I started shivering, maybe from the cold and maybe ..."

We woke to rain the following morning and returned to Glacier Lake.

Linda Thompson bouldering.

FOOD FOR COMMON FOLKS

Following his 600-mile trek through the Ragged Range and after spending about ten years hunting and trapping in the area, Dalziel observed that, *"By my calculations, a man such as myself, would need at least 100 pounds of grease or fat from a moose or bear to survive successfully for one winter."*

In preparation for our trip, I studied every word that the old-timers like the Raups, Dalziel, R.M. Patterson, Al Lewis and Albert Faille wrote about food and its importance to survival in that harsh and rugged environment. While we couldn't shoot a moose each week like they did, or carry a hundred pounds of fat, as Dalziel suggested, we knew we needed a lot of nutrition to keep our bodies warm and our minds sharp.

Since we dehydrated all our food, fat, which can't be dehydrated because it turns rancid, wasn't something we could use in our meals. As a substitute, we needed a good supply of carbohydrates, which we could carry. For protein, we de- and rehydrated lean ground beef and we also carried cheese and spicy sausage.

I also knew, as Lucy Raup said, breakfast was the most important meal and could determine the morale of the group for the entire day. We, like the old-timers, cooked rolled oats for most meals. Eggs, a common Canadian breakfast, can't be carried for a long period of time due to the threat of samonella poisoning and, to get a full meal, eggs are usually served with bacon and bread. We once carried canned bacon in our truck for roadside meals, but I haven't seen it on the shelves for a long time. Slab bacon is way too heavy and smelly to carry, and commercial bread, even with preservatives, goes stale within days.

The old-timers carried flour and made bannock instead of bread, but then they had the fat from the animals they shot in which to fry the bannock. We carried some fat for that purpose, but only because we were making hikes out of the Glacier Lake campsite and could store the fat there for our returns. When we fried our biscuits at Glacier Lake after we'd hiked for a few days, we couldn't believe how good they tasted. Not a crumb or drop of fat was left in the pan.

Our lunches, as I've said, were always cheese, crackers and highly concentrated sausage. The cheese would have been a luxury to the old-timers, but the sausage, as Al Lewis wrote in *Nahanni Remembered*, would be the same as the dried meat or jerky the old-timers made every time they shot a moose. Albert Faille, probably the most experienced of the bunch, brought pemmican with him, which he'd purchased from the Aboriginal people. To make pemmican, they used smoked meat or jerky added to fat or suet. They then threw in a handful of berries and compressed the lot into a patty.

High-fat chocolate bars are a great substitute for pemmican because, again, the sugar and fat in bars supply some warmth and energy. Trail mix should be loaded with carbohydrates rather than protein and used in the afternoons, when energy is really starting to fail.

Patterson loved preparing meals and was famous for his mulligan stew, which consisted of wild sage, red pepper, wild onions, dried potatoes, rice and leaves of Labrador tea, plus moose meat and/or bacon. If moose meat was scarce, he'd sometimes use a partridge. For us, we didn't plan any meals that had to be prepared from scratch.

Patterson was also famous for his porridge. In *Dangerous River* he wrote, "The porridge, let me explain, was no invalid dish, nor would it ever figure on the diet sheet of a slimming movie star: porridge as developed by me on the Nahanni consisted of a mixture of rolled oats and whole wheat, and into this was thrown a little salt, a large pat of butter, and a handful of seedless raisins. The finished product was served in a large bowl. On top of the porridge, I'd place a thin slice of cheese and the dish was topped off with a pouring of dried milk, mixed to the consistency of cream. A liberal sprinkling of brown sugar finished it off."

Patterson's porridge was just what he called, "A good foundation for the good breakfast to follow." After the porridge came, depending on what was available, "sheep liver and bacon, bannock, butter, marmalade and tea, topped with a bowl of raspberries and cream."

For carbohydrates, the old-timers had rice with them, and Patterson also used a lot of dehydrated potatoes. Rice (not rice noodles) doesn't absorb water as easily as flour, so it was safer to carry and easier to store. We also used rice or pasta noodles, or, like Patterson, dehydrated potatoes.

For emergencies, we carried a half-pound bag of dehydrated pea soup. It is thick, rehydrates almost instantly and is light to carry. On occasion, we used it for lunches when someone was exceptionally cold.

I am sure the old-timers would have loved to spike their tea or coffee with a shot of whiskey each night, or maybe they did but just didn't write about it. What Linda found (or maybe it was a con-job that I believed) was that, often, the body shuts down its response to hunger if it has been working much harder than usual. Small amounts of alcohol can and do stimulate the appetite, especially after a hard day. Believing that, we made it a habit, after camp was set up and while dinner was simmering, of having a pre-dinner cocktail to stimulate our appetites. We found it worked. I'm sure that if Dalziel had thought of it, he'd have taken an extra dog just to carry some medicinal schnapps.

CHAPTER 18

INTO THE CIRQUE

The morning after we arrived from our trip up Frost Creek was hot and sunny, which is unusual for the Cirque. The park's welcoming committee suggested that rather than having a rest day, we should go into the Cirque and utilize the good weather.

The committee told us that, just that year, the park workers had completed a trail from the lake to Fairy Meadows, the area in the Cirque guarded by Cathedral Mountain and where climbers gathered, watching and hoping the weather would clear so they could climb.

"The trail follows the one described in *Diary of a Lake*," said Andrea, one of the park officials. "You recommended coming down that way, through the forest. You don't cross the creek until you're in the meadow by the overhanging rocks."

I was glad to hear this. The original climb, as I described earlier, was up the talus slope below Cathedral, where rocks the size of pick-up trucks moved when pushed with a finger and free-moving scree flowed down in waves at the sound of approaching boots.

"You don't need to carry much water, because it shouldn't take much more than two or three hours to get up and you're near the creek all the way."

Tufa and travertine near Glacier Lake. Photo by Deb Hazell.

I failed to ask what "near" and "much more" meant. Coming down on my previous trip in 1999 had been so quick we didn't need water, and on this trip, I assumed the creek would always be within a two-minute walk off the trail.

We shook hands with the park people and eagerly headed up the trail, cameras clicking and Peggy singing—she had switched from the songs of the 1960s to the 1950s. Crossing Frost Creek was uneventful, but the second creek, just a few meters beyond, was covered with flowing orange travertine and tufa mounds that compelled us to drop our packs and explore. The formation of the tufa and travertine is caused by underground thermal activity. As the water travels upward, it passes through and dissolves limestone and siltstones. Once at the surface, the carbon dioxide in the water dissipates, leaving the lime precipitates to form the tufa and travertine. Generally, travertine is smoother than tufa, but we couldn't tell one from the other. The orange colour was caused by the water's reaction with hydrous iron oxide.

After an hour of exploring and photographing, we planted our packs on our backs and headed up the new trail. And up it was. Straight up. No switchbacks. And the sun was out. So were the wasps. Linda and I, being the oldest and slowest, were the ones on whom the wasps took their revenge after speedsters Peggy and Deb, using their hiking poles, had poked the nests hidden in the ground.

One wasp was so angry at being disturbed by the hikers that he came at Linda like a kamikaze suicide fighter-jet, buzzing straight for her forehead. I'm sure I saw him make a couple of circles before he hit dead center, pulled away and hit again.

Besides avoiding or not avoiding the wasps, Linda had another problem. She was thirsty. On the park's advice, we had decided to forgo the extra weight of carrying water. After three hours, we realized we were only about halfway to the meadows, and the sun was overhead, beating down through the trees.

We listened, but there was no sound of water running. Deb and Peg were ahead. I saw them drop their packs. They were in an opening and near the top. There had to be water. Linda, never a complainer, was red, slow and frowning. She and I both dropped our packs and sat on them, waiting for a rescue. Then I saw Deb coming back down the trail with a container, which I knew would be full of cold water. Linda drank like it was beer.

Peggy was sound asleep in the sun when we reached the creek. I wanted to join her, but we still had another hour before we would arrive at the meadow.

"It is a Hobbit House," Peggy cried after we crossed the creek and reached the first of the overhanging boulders, where we'd planned on camping. The gigantic rock had a slanted ceiling towards the back but covered a relatively level spot with enough room to make and eat a meal, at the upper section. The lawn in front was flat and large enough to pitch all four tents. And it overlooked a heaven-perfect view.

Our Hobbit House was half-occupied by a couple of American climbers from Oregon, Jason Luthy and Christian Thompson. They were here to climb Lotus Flower Tower, which had won the title of being the most challenging climb in the Cirque because its 2,000-foot southeast buttress is striking and similar to the Nose of El Capitan in Yosemite.

Jason Luthy and Christian Thompson shared the Hobbit duplex.

Jason had received an American Alpine Club "Live Your Dream" grant, which helped to pay the cost for him and Christian to get into the Cirque.

The grant, sponsored by North Face and "designed to help every-day adventurers take their abilities to the next level," is for an amount ranging between $200 and $1,000, depending on the dream. The goal of the participant must be difficult and at the edge of that person's physical and technical ability. Jason had drawn up an itinerary and budget and entered the contest. A few months later, he showed the letter announcing his success to his long-time climbing partner, Christian. Jason claimed that the sparkle in Christian's eye was a solid commitment that the trip would happen. They saved, trained, and dreamed. Finally, departure day arrived and they drove the endless 2,500 kilometers from Idaho up to what had been the destination of our drive, Finlayson Lake, on the Robert Campbell Highway.

According to Jason, the reality of getting into the Cirque didn't hit until they loaded the plane and lifted off Findlayson Lake. After all, they were from Oregon and had never climbed in Canada before. Once unloaded at Glacier Lake, they, too, thought the little hike to Fairy Meadows would be short and not too difficult, so they grabbed all their gear and headed up. Hours later, as dusk dimmed the imposing towers, they got out of the trees and passed the protective peak of Cathedral. Totally exhausted, they found a flat spot to pitch the tents and collapsed, removing only their boots.

After what seemed like just minutes, they were awakened by daylight shining through the tent walls and the sound of climbers grumbling as they passed.

"... consistently raining ... route is wet ... one team ... pancake mix in the food box ... more clouds drifting in ..."

"We've got 12 days ..."

"We need four ..."

They rolled over and slept again. Later that day, they looked around and saw the overhanging rock. They threw their gear into their packs and moved to the Hobbit House. After stacking a few more rocks here and there to make a table and a comfortable dividing wall, they made coffee and talked to a second group who, disheartened by the weather, were heading to the lake to wait for pick-up. The gossip was that just one team during the entire summer had managed to climb the Lotus.

Jason and Christian were sitting on the rock chairs, coffee mugs in hand, when we arrived.

"Mind if we share your duplex?" Deb asked and Jason nodded. We then pitched tents in the meadow and Linda put on the water for tea.

The northern sun dipped below the peak of Mount Ida to the southwest as we sipped our spiked tea and talked with Jason and Christian about other climbers who had done the tower. Suddenly, everyone went dead silent and watched as a wall of mist swirled up the same slope that we had hiked just hours before. The mist flooded Fairy Meadows until visibility was about ten meters. Even the bright green roof of the new multimillion-dollar compostable outhouse across the creek was invisible and the sounds of the campers' activities on the opposite side of the valley became muffled.

A million-dollar outhouse replaced a hole in the ground once the Park boundaries were expanded.

I'd seen weather collect at high peaks before. The rain that gathered at Mount Decoli, the highest mountain in the front range of Kluane National Park, forced us more than once to retreat to the comfort of a bed and breakfast. If we ever saw Mount Robson, the highest mountain in British Columbia's Rockies, not in cloud, we were compelled to stop and take a photo. And farther abroad, on a trip to Mount Illampu in the Bolivian Andes, we had been forced to cancel a ten-day hike because the weather had moved in, bringing rain, sleet and snow. Our guide was far too cold in his rubber-tire sandals and second-hand jacket to go farther up than the 5,000 meters that we were at.

But the Cirque's granite towers, dominated to the north by the second-highest mountain in the Northwest Territories, Mount Sir James McBrien, seemed to attracted more moisture than anything I'd ever seen.

I then decided to check out the toilet. I jumped across the creek, missing the grass by a foot, and got a boot full. As I sat in the composting outhouse, wringing out my sock, I looked out at Cathedral. The only comparison I could remember was at a hotel in China where the outhouse overlooked Mount Everest. The Cirque's new loo was designed by architect John Harrop, and with financial help from the Alpine Club of Canada, it was an improvement over the last time we were here, when there was no place to put excrement except under a rock—and most rocks had been taken!

Back at the Hobbit House, I finished my tea and climbed into bed, randomly opening *Diary of a Lake* to the section about the Pentagon team. They had given us an accurate description of the Frost Creek hike, so I assumed the rest of their information would be right on. Thomas had written, "We awoke that morning to the slow, steady beat of rain on our sleeping bags. And we looked out on a bleak wet world where heavily saturated clouds hung dark and threatening in the valley and the mountains in ominous swirling vapour ..."

Oh yes, I thought, as I tucked my book into the side pocket of my tent and drifted off to sleep to the rhythm of pattering rain.

The following morning, I awoke to the same sound and the same saturated clouds as Thomas had seen over eighty years ago. I pulled on all my rain gear and crawled out of the tent to make coffee. Also, like Thomas, I saw mountains in ominous swirling vapour. At the Hobbit House, our climbing neighbours were looking pretty glum.

But none of us felt like Thomas. We weren't climbing and we weren't, like the Pentagon team, on a seemingly endless quest through the wilderness.

We had a hot coffee and porridge, tucked a lunch into our packs and started our explorations of the valleys in the Cirque. Like the lake above Frost Creek, the rocks were huge, many not yet anchored by passing time, and the cloud cover obstructed our views. But there was no willow or alder.

"This is the Cirque of the Unhike-ables!!" Linda said over and over, as we struggled over rocks the size of bulldozers and down slopes steep enough to warrant the use of ropes. She was right. This was non-hike-able.

PURSUIT OF THE WALL

I stood watching the rain and read from *Diary* that when the Raups were at the lake studying the flora of the area they had recorded the daily temperatures. The maximum average daily temperature was 18.7° C (65.7° F) with a maximum of 28.6°C (83.5°F). The minimum average was 6.4° C (43.6° F), and the lowest they recorded was 0°C (32°F). Out of those sixty days, the rain fell on nineteen days.

"Okay, we've had our two days out of three of rain," said Linda. "The sun should soon be here. According to the official environmental report at Tungsten, just two valleys over, we should get about a foot of rain every year. I think we topped that in one day!"

And with that, the clouds broke, the rain stopped, and a sliver of blue contrasted with the grey. We had breakfast and packed up for a day of exploring. We'd hike to the farthest reach of the valley towards Lotus Flower Tower.

"I'll take the tarp," Deb said. "Just in case."

"Rain jacket," said Peggy. "Check."

"Umbrella ... check."

Christian grabbed his camera and clicked away as we proceeded up the valley and past a rock wall that, because of its shape, is called the Penguin.

"If it stays like this and the wall dries ..."

There was a crack of thunder and the rain started again. We didn't look back.

Silently we trudged through the rain, jumping from rock to rock across large pools of water and keeping our heads down against the wind. Near the entrance to the Lotus Flower Tower's valley, we stopped a moment and looked up. The mist swirled away from a straight granite wall, leaving us just enough time to gasp before the vapour returned.

Peggy Tobin maneuvering over large, slippery rocks in the pouring rain.

Being this close to the king of Canadian rocks, we hoped to see more, so we pulled out the tarp and made a shelter between a group of boulders. It was a tight fit for the four of us, but our tea was warm and our cheese and sausage filling, and occasionally, we could see the outline of the Lotus bobbing in and out of the fog. We watched. The rain fell harder and the mist got thicker. We waited until our fingers were numb and our noses dripped.

Disappointed with the weather, we returned to camp, where we found Jason and Christian tucked in, reading and listening to the monotonous drumming. This was their seventh day in the Cirque and they hadn't even pulled a piton out of their gear bag, let alone climbed. Instead, they had gone down to the cabin at Glacier Lake just for the exercise.

"How long did it take to climb back up?" Peggy asked.

"Two hours and eleven minutes."

"It took us two hours and twelve minutes!" Deb replied.

Since it was too early to prepare and eat dinner, we jumped across the creek and went over to see who was in the neighbouring hobbit house. A couple from Whitehorse had made a warm shelter by hanging tarps around their tents, thus preventing the wind from erasing any heat they might have generated while in their sleeping bags. Behind their tarps and tents was a kitchen, far more spacious than ours but still susceptible to the wind, whereas our kitchen was sheltered. The two from Whitehorse were, like everyone else, watching the sky.

We said hello to a group of non-talking, non-smiling Americans camped near the Whitehorse climbers and got a nod but no verbal response. The Americans were preoccupied with a gadget of a kind we hadn't seen before. Something buzzed above us. We stood close to the climber with the hand-held operating piece.

"That's a drone!" Linda yelled in surprise. The operator nodded.

But no matter how many questions we asked, or how insistent we became for an answer, our drone operators were not interested in telling us anything. They sort of waved us away and continued droning the surrounding cloud-covered peaks.

"They're the USA of the mountain—get it?" Linda asked. "Unfriendly silent Americans!"

"Would their drone flight be considered a new first?"

"Sort of like being the first to map the ground cover?"

"Or maybe they're delivering coffee to other guys on top of some wall?"

"Hardly."

We knew that it was illegal for manned or unmanned vehicles to take off or land in a national park without a Parks Canada Restricted Activity Permit. In the event of obtaining a permit, though, the drone would have to be used only for natural or cultural resource management, and the Unfriendly Silent Americans didn't seem to be doing anything like that. We felt it better not to confront them.

The Penguin, a perfect wall on which to practice climbing.

The following morning, as we lay in our tents, we realized something was missing. It was quiet and bright—no pit, pit, patter. Once up, we thought it might be a sunny day, although it was raining on the far side of the valley, toward Mount Ida. After discussion with our neighbours, our plan was to hike until mid-afternoon and then join them while they climbed the Penguin after it had dried—if it dried.

The Penguin is a wall rated at 5.12 by the American Yosemite Decimal System. Europeans were the first to establish a rating system. An Austrian mountaineer, Fritz Benesch, in the late 1800s developed a seven-point scale, with number one being the most difficult. In 1923, the German climber Willo Welzenback turned the rating scale around so zero was the easiest and the climbs were rated up to a four or five. In 1937, and around the time Lambert was maybe, hauling butt up Cathedral, the Sierra Club developed the system used now throughout North America.

These rating systems turned out to be very useful when exchanging information and reports about climbs. The ratings eventually expanded, so today there are seven major rock, four alpine, four ice and two aid-climbing systems used internationally. The main purpose of rating a climb is mostly to improve safety. It helps climbers choose a wall that is within their skill level, their time frame, and possible with the equipment they have at their disposal.

The easiest, Class 1, is a hiking scramble with no handholds—sort of what we were doing most of the time. Class 2 involves some scrambling and use of hands, which we certainly had done on a number of exploratory excursions since we'd been here. Class 3 requires climbing or scrambling frequently and the use of hands, but no technical equipment is required other than having a rope available. We moved to this degree of difficulty only once on this trip, at the top end of Frost Creek. Class 4 is where intermediate skill is required and where most climbers should have a rope. A fall at this level could be serious or fatal. The Class 5 category has numerous numbers after the decimal, and is where the really serious climbers want to live.

The Penguin and the Lotus are both 5.12, which means that rock shoes, along with excellent skills and strength, are required. Plus, extensive training in technical moves and techniques is essential before a climber tries something in this category.

What adds to the degree of difficulty in the Cirque is the weather and isolation. Should an accident happen, the chances of death increase tremendously, simply because rescue is not always possible due to weather. Even if a helicopter can get in, the flight out to a medical clinic would be a few hours at the least. And under the best of circumstances, a minimum of eight hours would be required before someone injured could get to a hospital.

After our morning of hiking, we arrived back at camp to find the boys had made cinnamon buns and were gracious enough to share. With blood sugar levels up, we all headed toward the Penguin, now dry and waiting. Gripping cameras, we perched ourselves on a huge, flat rock for a bird's-eye view of the climb.

Jason was the first to ascend, and according to him, the Penguin rises as a dihedral, where two walls meet at right angles, on the inside corner. In this case, the angle moves toward a prominent fin of rock resembling a Penguin's head. Jason harnessed in and Christian belayed. After pushing one foot against one side of the wall and the other foot against the other side, Jason shimmied, inch by inch, on the thin granite edges, to the base of the Penguin's neck. There he found small handholds that allowed him to grasp the rock well enough so he could pass up the Penguin's throat. At the top of the throat, he swung his arm over and grasped the beak of the bird. There, he hung by one arm. We cheered and yelled until he got back on the wall and belayed down.

Hearing our commotion, the Whitehorse crew came over, clutching ropes, pitons, gear and lunch, and we all encouraged Christian to climb. Sitting at our ringside seats across from the Penguin, we sat cameras poised and cheered with the enthusiasm of football fans. Christian placed his foot on the wall and all went silent. Each of us seemed to be hauling our bodies up the rock alongside of him. Christian fell, and we gasped. Luckily, Jason had a good hold of the belay rope. Christian climbed again, and he fell again. He slowly worked halfway up the throat and then moved quicker. Finally, like Jason, he swung his arm out and grabbed the bird's beak at the top. And of course, he got huge applause.

"That—is the hardest climb I've ever done!" Christian said, beaming, once he'd belayed down. I could see his hands trembling.

We left for Glacier Lake before Jason and Christian climbed the Lotus, but Jason sent me their account of the climb. Here is my rendition of their rendition.

JASON & CHRISTIAN 2015

The following morning, at dusk, the sun was rising, mist was gone, and the rain held off. They packed their gear and walked through the blooming wildflowers toward the Lotus, the real reason they had come.

Like so many desires in Jason's life, he said, climbing the Lotus was a subtle dream. Months and years had passed with little thought of getting into the Cirque. But then he'd see a photo of the parallel cracks stretching along a white headwall or watch a video, and again he'd imagine himself on that wall.

They ambled toward the flat face of the tower, each step making it seem to grow higher, straighter. The tower started wide at the base and tapered upward, ending in a squared-off summit. The obvious route was a single crack that ran almost 2,000 feet, cut only by a small ledge half way up.

According to Jason, they roped in at the base of the tower and began their upward climb. The first three pitches (each pitch is 20 feet) were soaking wet, but at the end of it they stepped around a roof and into the sun, where there was dry rock. The next set of pitches seemed to take hours, and it wasn't until 1 pm that they reached the ledge where others, with more time, could sleep. But rather than pitching a tent, Jason and Christian kept moving. For the next 1,000 feet they lifted into a vertical environment like they had never experienced before. With each pitch, they felt more wind, more sun and had better views of glaciers and future summits, although their currently desired summit still seemed like a lifetime away. Up and up they climbed.

And then, almost as an anticlimax, they realized that they had made it! They were on the top. The dream for a couple of American climbers had been realized. And they are just two among the hundreds who have tried and failed, tried and succeeded, and hundreds more who are still dreaming of the Lotus Flower Tower.

THE END

Until the early 1970s, the Cirque was popular only with North American climbers, but in 1972 mountain photographer Galen Rowell published a series of photos, and the international climbing community started arriving in droves. These foreigners, mostly Europeans or Japanese, have made three-quarters of the first ascents in the Cirque.

George Bell, a nationally acclaimed physicist and dedicated climber, has summited numerous peaks, including K2, the most difficult mountain in the world. About the Cirque he wrote:

If the Alaska Highway ran right past the Cirque of the Unclimbables it would undoubtedly be much more popular. Each morning, a stream of climbers would issue from the campground up well-trodden trails to the base of each wall. Experts would be competing for speed records on the Lotus Flower Tower and Proboscis. Fairy Meadow would be eroded by deep troughs from the constant foot traffic. In short, the Cirque would be even more like Yosemite. Thus, perhaps the most important aspects of the Cirque are the ways in which it differs from Yosemite: its isolated location, and the narrow windows of good weather. Any climber entering the Cirque today feels much the same sense of awe and remoteness that the first explorers to the region felt more than half a century before.

INDEX

A
Above the Falls, 100
Aboriginal, 29, 37, 52, 201
Addison, W.D., 27, 37, 43–45, 51–52
Agriculture Canada, 164
Ahti, Teuvo, 112
Airways Belanca, 167
Alaska, 30, 67,
Alaska Highway, 5, 155, 217
Alberta, 29, 100, 103, 105, 111, 114, 116–117, 195
Albuquerque, 124
Aleutian Islands, 123
Alpine Club, American/Canadian 108, 206, 209
Alpine Journal, 151, 160
American Museum of Natural History, 103, 107

America/ns, 104, 110–11, 123, 164, 173, 175, 188, 206, 212–13, 217
American Yosemite Decimal System, 214
Anderson, Oscar, 31
Andes, 209
Anthony, Garnet, 167
Aonica, David, 167
Appian Way, 143–144
arctic grayling, 97
Arctic Ocean, 142
Armstrong, Joanne, 5, 7, 14, 34
Arnold, Edward, 176
Arnold Arboretum, 112
Asia/Asian, 96, 108, 148
Athabasca River, 48
Athabasca, Lake, 108
Atlas Explorations, 85
Australia, 56

Austrian, 214
Aviation Museum of Alberta, 29, 37,
Awareco, 45

B
B.C., 30, 109, 174, 187
Bailar, John Christian, 101, 152, 154, 156–158, 167,
Banff, 96
Bates, Carrol, 104
Bear Lake, 45, 106
beaver, 38, 52
bear, 57, 94–95, 103, 111, 144
Beaver plane, 187–188
Bell, George, 178, 217
Benesch, Fritz, 214
Bennett Creek, 40, 55, 63
Berdahl, Ron, 85
Berglund, Alex, 8
Bering Sea, 123
Bernays, Dave, 173–174
Berton, Pierre, 103, 106
Bhopol, India, 83
Biedermann, Stephan, 134, 136–139, 142, 144, 169,
Harthon, Bill, 178
Billiton Metals, 66
Bittenger, D., 174

Black Wolf Creek, 34
Bolivian Andes, 209
Bologna Creek, Icefields, Valley, 121–122, 125–128, 182, 193–4
Bolyard, Dudley, 101, 124, 127, 152–161, 174, 182
Book and Record Depository (see University of Alberta), 100, 115–117, 195
Borden Creek, 63
Bors, Stan, 24, 72
Bostock, Dr Hugh, 123, 153
Bothwell, Robert, 106
Bowers, Ray, 31–32
Boynton, Ted, 105, 108, 110
Bradford-Andrew, Rebecca, 100
Bradford, Sherry, 27, 36, 43, 45, 53, 130
Brewis, Steve, 102
Brintnell Creek/Lake, 108–109, 121, 128–129, 131, 135, 146–148, 164, 167, 175, 190
Brintnell Glacier, 109–110, 126, 134, 144, 148, 154, 156, 166–167, 175, 182, 189–191
Brintnell, Leigh, 107–109, 170
Brodell, Hugo, 85
Buchan, John, 102–103
Buckingham, Bill, 101, 175–177

Bulkley Range, 174
Burbidge, Moss, 35
Burton, Sir Richard Francis, 96
Bushwhack, 59, 61, 82, 135–136, 141–142, 148, 189, 193

C
CBC, 167
Californian, 31
Campbell, Milt, 49, 51
Canada/Canadian, 8, 33, 35, 43–44, 47, 69, 84, 102, 104, 106, 108, 110, 115, 123, 153, 173, 180, 207
Canada geese, 109
Canada Tungsten Mining Corporation Ltd.,/Cantung, 8, 10, 68, 70
Canadian Exploration Ltd., 84
Canadian Forestry Service, 180
Canadian Geographical Journal, 109, 111, 123
Canadian Heritage River, 179
Canadian Museum of History, 104
Canadian Museum of Nature, 104
Canadian Pacific Airlines, 36
Canadian Parks Service, 169
Canadian Rockies, 209
Canadian Wildlife Service, 163–164, 167, 180
Canex Aerial Exploration Ltd., 84
Canex Placer, 85
Canol Pipeline, 64, 79, 99
Canol Road, 7, 191
caribou, 69, 82, 85, 156, 164
Caribou River, 38, 41, 47–49, 52, 180–183
Cathedral Mountain, 100, 103, 108–110, 148, 151–152, 155, 159–160, 167, 175, 191–193, 203, 207, 209, 214
Centennial Mines & Canadian Exploration, 84
Champlain Oil, 106
Chihong Canada, 69
Chile, 187
China, 8, 67, 209
Chinese, 8, 44, 69
Churchill, Corporal David, 42
Cirque of the Unclimbables, 96–97, 100, 108–110, 122–123, 133–135, 144, 148, 151–152, 161, 168–171, 173–175, 177, 180, 183–192, 203, 206–207, 209–210, 212, 215–217
Cladina moss, 91, 122

Clark, Bill, 33, 40, 47, 49, 51–52, 96, 151
Coal River, 33
Cochrane, 44
Colonel Mountain, 107–108
Colorado, 125, 154
Congo River, 113
Copper Ridge Explorations, 66
Cormack, brothers, Bill/George, 28, 36–48, 51–55, 114, 164, 170
Cowan, Ian McTaggart, 29
Cowan, Patrick, 29
Cranberry Rapids, 31
Cream of Wheat, 159
Crooked River, 104
Cryptogamic Botany, 112
Curtis Robin, 29, 35, 54
Cygnus Mines, 66
Cypress Hills, 169

D

D'Arcy, Ray, 173–174
Dahadinni River, 35
Dall Lake, 35
Dall sheep, 85, 111, 181
Dalziel Airways, 167
Dalziel, George, 27–45, 47–48, 51–55, 59, 61, 100, 111, 114, 121, 123–124, 126, 130–131, 133–134, 152, 155, 164, 167, 170, 173–174, 183, 200, 202
Dangerous River, 5, 33, 201
Dawson City, 170
Day, W., 164
Deadman Valley, 33, 42
Dease Lake, 31
Dease River, 31
Deck, Donalee, 168–171
Decoli, Mount, 209
Dehcho First Nation, 179
Dene, 68–69, 112, 179
Denmark (Danish), 71, 87, 134
Dept. of Indian Affairs & Northern Development (DIAND), 70
Dept. of Resources, Wildlife & Economic Dev., 183
Depression, 28, 37, 44
Devil's Canyon, 30
Diary of a Lake, 100, 131, 203, 209–210
Dillon, Marshal, 18
Distant Early Warning Line (DEW Line), 123
Dodge City, 18
Dog Leg (Dogleg) Creek/River, (see Bologna Creek)
Donjek Glacier, 186

Douglas M. Pinlott Award, 180
Dow Chemical Co., 83–84
Dozer Lake, 83, 90–91
Dresden, Germany, 14
Drill Creek Pass, 91
Drone, 189, 212–213
Duke River, 186
Duke University, 112
Durham, North Carolina, 112

E
Earth Sciences Information Centre, 163
Edmonton, 35, 37, 39, 44–45, 115, 163, 180
Edmonton Journal, 124, 128
Egyptian, 59
El Capitan, 174, 206
Eldorado, 106
Eldorado mine, 106, 110, 151
Envirocon Ltd., 85
Environmental Assessment Board, 69
Eppler, Bill, 40, 47, 49, 51–56, 100, 114, 133, 171
Europe/European, 43, 148, 169–170, 214, 217
Everest, Mount, 209
Expatriate Resources, 66

F
Faille, Albert, 6, 12, 34, 38, 49, 51, 53–55, 99–100, 183, 200–201
Fairhurst, Carol, 134, 136–137, 142–143, 145–146, 149
Fairy Meadows, 148, 170, 175, 203, 207–208, 217
Fang, 155
Farlow Herbarium, 112
Faroe Islands, 123
Faubion, Kelley, 187
Field, Poole, 28, 47, 54, 169–170
Fifty Classic Climbs in North America, 178
Figure Eight Rapids, 6
Finland, 112
Finlayson Lake, 184, 187–189, 207
First Canyon, 168
First Nations, 28, 63–64, 68, 99, 170, 179, 181, 189
Firth River, 47
Fishing Lake, 32
Flat Lakes, 7, 17, 19, 24–25, 27–28, 37–38, 40–42, 51, 57–58, 64–65, 72, 76, 82, 88, 95–97, 99, 134, 136, 139, 176, 180, 184, 191–192

INDEX

Flat River, 17, 28, 34, 38, 47–49, 54–56, 63–65, 68, 96–97, 133–138, 161, 164, 180, 182–184, 191–192
Flight of the Red Beaver, 27
Flint Glacier, 126, 135, 182
Flood Creek, 42
Flook, D.R., 48, 155, 160, 163–167, 194–195
Fool's River, 140
Fork Creek, 73
Fort Liard, 46
Fort Nelson, 45, 47
Fort Norman, 33, 35, 59
Fort Simpson, 28, 30, 35, 37–39, 42, 45–47, 54, 63, 108, 151, 163–164, 167, 183
Fort Smith, 37, 180
Frost Creek, 108, 115, 121, 125, 166–167, 192–193, 198, 203–204, 209–210, 214
Frost, Tom, 178

G

Gallwas, Jerry, 177
Geodetic Survey of Canada, 108
Geological Survey of Canada, 153
German/Germany, 134, 214
Gibson, Rex, 174
Gilmore Archeological Site, Sask., 169

Glacier Lake, 36, 40–41, 52–55, 97, 99–101, 103–104, 106–112, 114–116, 119, 121, 123–124, 126, 129, 131, 133–134, 148, 152–153, 155, 164, 167–171, 173–175, 180, 182–185, 188, 192, 194, 198–200, 204, 207, 212, 216
goat, 111, 181, 198
Godsell, Philip H., 27
Gold Creek, 63
Goodwin, George Gilbert, 101, 107–110, 112, 198
Goonetilleke, Hash, 187
gopher, 78
Goulet, Father, 46
Governor General of Canada, 102, 110
Graham, Constable, 54
Grand Central Station, 159
Grasslands National Park, 169
Gray, P., 104–105
Great Bear Lake, 106
Great Slave Lake, 104, 108, 112
Green, Graham, 103
Greenland, 123
Greenmantle, 102
Grizzly Lake, 34–35
Guthrie Creek, 73

H

Haines, 67
Half Dome, Mount, 177
Harper, Stephen, 68
Harris, John, 5, 7, 9, 11, 15, 17–18, 24–25, 39, 57–60, 66, 71, 74, 76–79, 82, 84, 87–90, 93–95, 100, 123, 133–134, 137–139, 141–142, 144–145, 148, 184, 186–187,
Harrison Pass, 15
Harrison Smith, Mount, 108–109, 170, 175, 193
Harrop, John, 209
Harvard University, 112
Harvey, Jacque, 134
Hay River, 167
Hazell, Deb, 186–187, 192, 195–199, 202, 204–205, 208, 211–212
Helsinki University, 112
Hendricks, Sterling, 101, 173–174
Herschel Island, 47
Herschel Archeological Site, Sask., 169
Hilliard, Harold, 103
Hole-In-The-Wall Creek, Lake, Valley, 34, 42, 61, 96, 176, 180, 182
Horseshoe Bay, 29
Howard's Pass, 61, 64–69, 71, 74–76, 97, 134, 140, 181–182, 184, 191
Hubbard, Donald, 101, 173–174
Hudson's Bay, 33
Hudson's Hope, 105, 113
Huey, Mount, 170
Hyland River, 9, 13, 15

I

Ice Dome Peak, 157, 159
Iceland, 123
Ida, Mount, 107–108, 110, 135, 144–145, 147, 156, 167, 208, 214
Idaho, 207
Illampu Mount, 209
Imperial Oil, 106, 108
India, 83–84, 95
Indigenous, 35, 46, 70
Indigenous Affairs and Cultural Heritage, 169
International Petroleum Co. Ltd., 108
Inuit, 112
Irvine Creek, 34, 49, 51, 53–55
Italy, 144

J

James McBrien, Sir, Mount, 161, 176–177, 193, 209
Japanese, 96, 217
Jarvis Pass, 109
Jennings, H. Dr., 163
Johnson, Albert, 35
Jorgenson, Martin, 28

K

K2, 217
Kakwa Provincial Park, 109
Kaska Dene Nation, 68–69, 170
Kiev, Ukraine, 43,
Kilgour, Glen, 167
King, Michael, 134, 138–139, 145
Klim milk, 115
Klondike/er, 99
Kluane Air, 184, 187–188, 190
Kluane National Park, 5, 71, 108, 134, 186–187, 209
Kor, Layton, 177
Kraus, Gus, 6, 33, 40, 42, 47–49, 52, 55, 104, 164–165, 167,
Kraus Hotsprings, 168–169
Kraus, Mary, 6,
Kuskula Creek, 15, 17, 19, 96, 134, 139–140

L

La Bine, Gilbert, 106
Lac La Biche, 37, 48
LaFave, Warren, 190
LaGreca, Scott, 112
Lambert, Howard Fredrick, 101, 108–109, 113, 151–152, 160, 174, 214
Lazenby, Richard, 134, 137, 139, 142, 144–146
Leckie Award, 67
Lened Creek, 83–85, 91–92, 182, 184
Lewis, Al, 27, 38–39, 41, 52, 122, 200–201
Liard Band, 28
Liard River, 28, 30–33, 43, 45, 64, 97, 133, 142, 164, 170, 183
Little Bear River, 46
Little Nahanni River, 61, 65, 72–74, 83, 87–90, 95–97, 180, 182, 184, 191
Live Your Dream, 206
Living on the Brink, 152, 161
Lockport Archeological Site, Man., 169
Logan, Mount/Mountains, 108–109, 151, 153–154, 168, 174
Lomar, John, 45, 48–49, 51–52

London, Jack, 33, 63, 65
Lotus Flower Tower, 174–175, 177–178, 206, 208, 210–212, 214, 216–217
Lower Post, 31–33
Luthy, Jason, 206–208, 212, 215–216

M
MIT, 174
McCarthy, Jim, 177–178
McClellan, Catherine, 170
McConachie, Grant, 29, 36
McCracken, Dick, 177
McLeod brothers, 33, 40, 42, 47, 49
McLeod Creek, 33, 47, 51, 63
McLeod, Willie, 42
McMillan Air, 109
McMillan Lake, 33
McMillan, Stan, 109
Mac Creek, 72
Mackenzie Air, 107
Mackenzie Mountains, 101, 109, 111, 123, 153, 156, 164, 181
Mackenzie River, 30, 33, 35, 46, 59, 64, 67, 142, 170
Mackenzie Valley Land & Water Board, 70

MacMillan Pass, 64, 66, 69–70, 80, 191
Mactung, 69
Mad Trapper, 35
Manhattan Project, 106
Manitoba, 169
Marble Mountain, 155
March Creek, 74–75
Marcello's, 187
marmot, 78, 144
marten, 30, 38–39, 52, 164, 183
Martyn, Howell, 46, 101–102, 107, 110, 118, 122–129, 131, 152–156, 158, 165–166, 170, 177, 193
Martyn, Mrs. 124, 128, 131, 160
Mary River, 180
Mason, Bill, 87
Mather, Peter, 102
May, Wop, 35, 42
Mekong River, 113
Melrose, Saskatchewan, 44
Meilleur River, 180
mink, 31
Milton, John, 176
Miner's Junction, 9–10
Mirror Lake, 15, 17, 138–139, 184
moose, 28, 31, 49, 85, 109, 119, 181, 194, 198, 200–201

Moose Ponds, 97, 99, 134, 184
Monaghan, Hugh, 164
Morrison brothers, 31
Moscow, 43
Mountain Meadow, 102
Mountain First Nations, 170
Mulholland, Jack, 47, 49, 54,
Mulholland, Joe, 40, 47, 49, 51–56, 100, 114, 133, 171
muskoxen, 104
Mutt, 31–32
My Old People Say, 170
Mysterious North, The, 103

N

Naha First Nation, 33
Nahanni, 5, 27, 45
Nahanni Butte, 28, 35, 39, 40–42, 45, 47, 52–54, 63, 167, 170, 179
Nahanni National Park, 5, 9, 68, 96, 163, 169, 179
Nahanni Range Road, 7–10, 68, 71, 87, 135, 140
Nahanni Remembered, 38–39, 201
Nahanni Revisited, 27,
Nahanni River (South), 5–7, 17, 34, 42, 45, 48–49, 55, 61, 63–65, 73, 79, 83, 88–90, 97, 100, 102, 108–109, 113–114, 121, 126–129, 131, 133–134, 142, 164, 168–170, 179–184, 191
Nance, Harry, 152, 154, 156
National Archives, 163
National Film Board, 6
National Museum of Canada, 104, 163–164
Natural History Magazine, 110
New Hampshire, 174
New Haven, 124
New York, 96, 107, 109, 149, 152, 159
Nipawin Dam Archeological Site Heritage Study, 169
Nirvana, Mount, 161, 176
Norman Wells, 46, 79
North Again for Gold, 106
North America, 8, 101, 169, 175, 214, 217
North American Tungsten/ Nortung, 8, 69–70
North Atlantic, 123
North Carolina, 112
North, Dick, 33, 56
North Face, 207
North Shore Mountains, 29
North West Mounted Police, 170

North Vancouver, 30, 37
Northern Abandoned Mine Reclamation, 70
Northern Traders, 46
Northwestern Explorations Ltd., 8
Northwest Territories/NWT, 6–8, 15, 30, 33–34, 38, 45, 52, 70, 104, 161, 164, 176–177, 180,
NWT Division of Tourism, 6
NWT Water's Act, 70
Norwegian, 28

O

Ohio, 103, 124
Oregon, 134, 190, 206–207
Ottawa, 106, 153, 179
Ovis dalli, 181

P

Pacific Coast, 108
Pacifica Resources, 66–67
Page, Ron, 167
Parks Canada/Parks Service, 48, 68, 168–169, 179, 184, 213
Parsnip River, 104–105
Patterson, R.M., 5, 28, 33, 42, 54, 63–65, 99, 112, 200–202
Peace Hydro Dam, 104

Peace River, 105
pemmican, 201
Penguin, Mount, 211, 213–215
Pennsylvania, 67
Pentagon, 122–123, 152, 154–155, 160, 193, 209–210
Peterson, Pete, 111
Phoenix, Arizona, 122
Pic Magazine, 103
Pilots of the Purple Twilight, 27
Pitt, Alex, 22
Pitt, Gerald, 19–20, 22–24, 61, 72, 83, 95–96, 136
Pitt, Natasha, 22
Pitt, Terri, 22, 72, 95–97, 136
Placer Dome Development Ltd., 65–66
Playfair Mining, 85
Plymouth Peak, 155
Point Atkinson, 29
Poland, 24, 43
poppy, 24, 58
Porcupine Bar, 31
porcupine, 13, 38
Port Hope, 106
Potato Hill, 77–78
primus stove, 159
Prince Edward Island Highlanders, 103

Prince George, 9, 14, 104, 109, 134
Prince George Citizen, 22
Proboscis, Mount, 144, 175–177, 217
prussic knot, 158

R

Rabbit River, 32, 37
Rabbitkettle Hotsprings, Lake, River, 19, 34, 37–38, 41, 52–53, 61, 99–101, 110, 114, 134–135, 140–143, 161, 171, 176, 182–183, 190
Raft Creek, 34
Ragged Range, 17, 23, 101, 103, 108–109, 174, 182–183, 200
Raup, Carl, David, Hugh Miller, Lucy, 101, 112–120, 156, 170, 182, 194–195, 200, 210
Red Baron, 35
Red Mountain, 108, 193, 198
Red Wing, 156–157
Redstone River (south), 35
Richardson, Bernie, 29
Riding Mountain National Park, 169
Robert Campbell Highway, 7, 9–10, 68, 187, 207

Roberts, George, 108–109, 151–152
Robbins, Royal, 177
Robson, Mount, 209
Rollog, Ollie, 46, 167
Root River, 35
Ross, Jim, 105–106, 108, 110–111,
Ross River, 28, 67, 191
Rowell, Galen, 102, 217
Royal Canadian Air Force, Royal Air Force, 35, 123
Royal Canadian Mounted Police (RCMP), 7, 10, 28, 30, 40–41, 47, 52, 54–55
Royal Geographical Society/ *Journal*, 103, 111, 123
Russian, 43, 46, 67, 123

S

St. Andrews Dam, Lockport Archeological Site, Man. 169
St Elias Range, 108
St George's Private School, 29
Saskatchewan, 37, 44, 169
Saskatchewan Research Council, 169
Savage, Mount, 176
Schulte, Matthias, 14

Scotter, George W, 101, 163, 167, 180
Seal, Daryl, 43
Selwyn Chihong, 68
Selwyn Mountains, 85, 183
Selwyn Resources, 67, 69
Seneca Rocks, 174
Servas, 14
Shamp, Dick, 122–131, 152, 154, 193
Shaw, T.E.G., 6
Shearer, Ida M., 106, 108–110
sheep, 35, 85, 104, 111, 181, 202
Shelf Lake, 122
Sherrick, Mike, 177
Sick Heart River, 102
Sidney Dobson, Mount, 101, 109, 126, 135, 143–144, 153–154, 182, 190
Sierra Club, 214
Sikanni River, 105
Simmons, Norman M., 180
Simmons, Hilah L., 180
Simon Fraser University, 29
Simpson Air, 134, 183
Siwash, 38
Skagway, 67
skin boats, 28, 40, 53–54
Skinboat Lakes, 37, 47, 180

Skull Creek, 42
Slave River, 112
Slim Raider, 167
Smith, Harrison, 108–109, 170, 175
Smithers, BC, 174
Snow Chute, 155
Snyder, Colonel Harry Michener, 103–113, 115, 123, 133, 151, 153, 163–164, 166–167, 170, 193–194, 198
Snyder, Dorothy, 106, 108
Snyder, Louise (Mrs), 108, 111, 164
Snyder Range, 107–108
Soper, Jim, 101, 112, 114, 119–120
South Fork, 144
South Nahanni River, 6–7, 34, 54, 61, 63–64, 79, 83, 97, 121, 134, 168, 170, 183–184
Soviet, 123
Spectra Natural Gas, 67
Split Glacier, 145
spruce, 61, 107, 115, 141, 193
squirrel, 72, 78
Stanier, Jack, 33, 47
Steel Creek, 64–65, 74, 76, 88
Stein, Karl, 109, 113, 152
Stewart, B.C., 67

Stewart Cassiar Highway, 187
Stewart, R.C., 164
stick man, 32, 52
Stikine River, 31
Stonemarten Lake, 42
Sunblood Mountain, 42
Sundre, Alberta, 105–106, 111
Surdam, Lew, 176
Sutcliff, Cam, 188–189, 191
SWAT, 24
Sykes, Reverend, 29

T
Taylor, George, 51
Tepee, 35, 111–112,
Telegraph Creek, 3
Territorial Lands Act, 70
Thirty Nine Steps, 102
Thomas, Jack, 105
Thomas, Norm, 46, 102, 118, 122–129, 131, 152, 154, 193–194, 196, 209–210
Thompson, Christian, 206–208, 211–212, 215–216
Thompson, Linda, 116, 185–186, 192–193, 196, 199, 202, 205, 208, 210, 212–213
Tlogotsho Plateau, 180
Toad River, 45–46

Tobin, Peggy, 187–189, 191–192, 196, 198–199, 204–206, 211–212
Toronto, 134
Travertine, 204–205
Trudeau, Charles-Emile, 106
Trudeau, Pierre Elliot, 6, 106, 179
Truesdell, A.W.M., 41, 47, 52
Tuchitua River, 9, 12
Tucson, Arizona, 112
Tufa, 204–205
Tungsten, 7–10, 12, 17–18, 23, 61, 64, 67–71, 84–85, 88, 95–97, 133–136, 139, 145, 169, 180, 183–186, 190–191, 210
Tungsten Hotsprings, 20
Tungsten John, 100
Turner, Dick, 5, 27, 43, 45, 52–55, 133
Tweedsmuir, Lord/Baron, 102, 106, 110, 151

U
Ukrainian, 43–44
UNESCO, 180
Union Carbide, 61, 83, 85, 87, 92, 95, 134
United States, 106, 112, 177
United States Geological Survey, 122

United Nations, 180
United Nations Environmental Programme, 181
University of Alberta, 29, 100, 114, 116–117, 195
University of Calgary, 112
University of Colorado, 154
University of Manitoba, 169
University of New Mexico, 124
University of Regina, 169

V
Vancouver, 29–31, 37, 56, 67, 69, 187
Vancouver College, 30
Vancouver Public Library, 7, 84
Vandaele, Harry, 38, 41, 49
Veale, Ron, 68
Virginia, 174
Virginia Falls, 42, 54, 108–109, 167, 183
Vingborg, Elsebeth, 15, 71, 76–77, 79–80, 82, 87–90, 93–95, 134, 137, 139, 142–143

W
WWI, 35
WWII, 79
Walsh, Shea, 9, 11, 15, 17–20, 57–60, 71, 134, 141
Washington, DC, 122, 124
Watson Lake, 7, 14, 24, 82, 121–122, 124, 126, 154–155, 160, 187–188
Weaver, John L, 181
Welzenback, Willo, 214
Wexler, Arnold, 101, 173–175
Whitehorse, 79–80, 167, 189, 212, 215
Whitesitt, Larry, 27
Who's Who in America/Canada, 106, 115
Williston Lake, 104
Wilson, Mount, 79–80, 184
Wings of the North, 6
Winnipeg, 44, 169
Wisconsin Age, 179
Wittington, Andy, 56
wolf/wolves, 31–32, 52, 55, 78, 181
wolverine, 38
Wolverine Air, 134
Wood Buffalo National Park, 108, 112
World Conservation Monitoring Centre, 181
Wrangell, Alaska, 30–31

Y

Yale Climbing/Mountaineering Club/Team, 112, 122–123, 125, 131, 144–145, 152–155, 160–161, 164, 167, 173
Yale University, 124–125, 153–154
Yellowhead Pass, 109
Yellowknife, 45–46, 106–107, 111
Yellowknife Blade, 106
Yntema, George, 101, 152, 154–155, 157–158, 166–167
Yosemite, 174, 177, 206, 214, 217
Yukon, 5, 15, 28, 30, 33, 37–38, 48, 64, 67, 69–70, 97, 124, 164, 169, 187
Yukon Government, 78
Yukon Highway, 13
Yunnan Chihong Zinc and Germanium Co. Ltd., 67, 69

Z

Zenchuk Creek, 19, 42, 58–61, 134–135, 141, 183
Zenchuk, Nazar, 28, 37–39, 41–49, 52, 55–56, 58, 60, 110–111, 164
Zenchuk, Platal, 43
Zenchuk, Orel Packla, 43
Zoltai, Stephen C., 180

RELATED TITLES

27 Years Off-grid in a Wilderness Valley

The Power of Dreams tells the story of a couple, already in their 40's, who uprooted themselves from urban life to follow their dream of living in the wilderness. They settled in a remote mountain valley called Precipice Valley, part of the ancient trade route linking B.C.'s Chilcotin plateau to the Pacific Coast. Surrounded by mountain vastness they lived there for nearly three decades, much of it in near-total isolation. Their dreams sustained them while they carved out a lifestyle that was both rewarding and challenging.

The Power of Dreams
Neads, Dave & Rosemary

978-0-88839-718-8 [paperback]
978-0-88839-742-3 [epub]
5½ x 8½, sc, 246pp

$24.95

A trilogy of stories by the Edwards family about their fascinating life in the Bella Coola area.

Often called "The Crusoe of Lonesome Lake," because of a best-selling book written by the American journalist Leland Stowe, Edwards has gone on to live at least one more life and reveals himself to be a pioneer of a breed that no longer exists. Best known for his almost single-handed rescue of the trumpeter swans from extinction in North America, Edwards now related in his own words other aspects of his long, varied life, including experience with his missionary parents in India, as a telegraph operator under fire in World War I and his eventual return to Lonesome Lake.

Ralph Edwards of Lonesome Lake
Gould, Ed & Ralph Edwards

978-0-88839-100-1 [paperback]
5½ x 8½, sc, 296pp

$19.95

other Canadiana titles from HANCOCK HOUSE PUBLISHERS

Burnt Snow
Kieran Moore
978-0-88839-309-8
6 x 9 sc, 272 pp
$24.95

Incredible Gang Ranch
Dale Alsager
978-0-88839-211-4
5½ x 8½, sc, 448 pp
$29.95

Flying to Extremes
Dominique Prinet
978-0-88839-145-2
5½ x 8½, sc, 280 pp
$24.95

Fire into Ice
Vern Frolick
978-1-55192-334-5
6 x 9, sc, 354 pp
$24.95

Bush & Arctic Pilot
Al Williams
978-0-88839-167-4
5½ x 8½ sc, 256 pp
$24.95

Mountain Ranch at the End of the Road
T. Hook & G. Brumbelow
978-0-88839-056-1
5½ x 8½, sc, 166 pp
$24.95

Descent into Madness
Vern Frolick
978-0-88839-026-4
5½ x 8½, sc, 361 pp
$24.95

Outposts & Bushplanes
Bruce Lamb
978-0-88839-556-6
5½ x 8½, sc, 208 pp
$17.95

Heritage Churches of the Indigenous Peoples of British Columbia
Ken Perry
978-0-88839-074-5
8½ x 11 sc, 240pp
$39.95

Hancock House Publishers
19313 0 Ave, Surrey, BC V3Z 9R9
www.hancockhouse.com
sales@hancockhouse.com
1-800-938-1114

www.ingramcontent.com/pod-product-compliance
Lightning Source LLC
Chambersburg PA
CBHW070733160426
43192CB00009B/1418